silkscreen now

Why do women earn only 62% of what men make?
and we work twice as hard!
Ludicrou
Some still dont believe in

Peach Berserk's Silk Screen NOW

with tips and tricks to make YOU a silkscreen star!

KINGI CARPENTER with **ANNALISA DANOWSKI**

Kingi and Annalisa dedicate this book to their fathers, much loved and much missed: Major-General Frederick Stanley Carpenter and Eugeniusz Danowski.

Published in 2008 by
Peach Berserk
507 Queen Street West
Toronto ON, M5V 2B4
(416) 504-1711

12 11 10 09 08   1 2 3 4 5

LIBRARY AND ARCHIVES CANADA CATALOGUING IN PUBLICATION

Carpenter, Kingi, 1962–
Silkscreen now / Kingi Carpenter and Annalisa Danowski.

Includes index.
ISBN 978-0-9810178-0-8

1. Screen process printing. I. Danowski, Annalisa, 1966– II. Title.

TT273.C37 2008   686.2'316   C2008-903717-0

Design: Ingrid Paulson
Photography: Nicole Brayshaw-Bond, Jocelyn Lee-Bun

Printed in Canada

table of contents

introduction

← EIFFEL FOR YOU:

This one is my absolutely very first, official, commercial print. I had been to Paris as a teenager, and couldn't believe that they didn't sell dresses with the Eiffel Tower on them! I designed this print for my trip to Paris in 1986. If the Parisians weren't going to sell me those dresses, then I would make some and sell them to the Parisians. I brought a garbage bag full of "Eiffel for You" print dresses to the foot of the Eiffel Tower itself and attempted to sell them. I sold **one**. To a tourist stall operator in the metro station. For half price. There's a happy ending, though: "Eiffel For You" became one of my best-selling prints, for everything from wedding dresses to upholstery fabric to underwear. A peachy secret: You may notice that the word "Eiffel" is misspelled a couple of times on this print... well, **you** may notice. I didn't until at least a year later when a customer pointed it out!

My name is Kingi, and I am a Misfit.

I was fired from fourteen "normal" jobs before I even turned 25. When I started Peach Berserk, my fashion company, I had no money or business training. I hadn't thought any of it through — I just knew I was sick of working for other people, following rules I didn't agree with, not being free to do things my own way. I realized that my only hope for a reasonable job was to work for myself. And oh yeah, I was tired of being fired. My bosses said that I didn't project their corporate image. I dished up extra portions; I wouldn't dish the corporate line when it meant I had to lie. I multitasked when they wanted me to focus. I handed out my own business cards to their customers and my high heels ruined their floors. But I think I've succeeded *because* I project my own image, revel in the chaos, give away free stuff, and wear supercute shoes. I make constant use of my Misfit super-powers. We misfits have great imaginations and strong visions of what we want, not what other people think we should want. Whatever we do, we overdo. We rebel, shake up the routine, and while that makes us nightmare employees, we are dream entrepreneurs.

I first discovered screen printing at art school, way, way back in 1985, two years before I started Peach Berserk. I signed up for a Surface Design class, having absolutely no idea how silkscreens worked, but I had just been to Paris, and thought that the world (and I) needed dresses covered in huge Eiffel Towers — amazingly, nothing like this was available in Paris at the time! What followed next was as close to a religious experience as I have ever had: I laid my screen down on a piece of fabric, squished some ink across with a squeegee, and lifted the frame to see the resulting print. All of my favourite things converged beneath that magic screen: my love of drawing, pop art, Paris, and of course fabric, because fabric means fashion to me.

I've always loved fashion, drawing and silkscreening, and I wanted to do them all my way. I had a vision of all my gorgeous handprinted dresses, with my drawings on them, hanging in my own gorgeous store. So I made it happen, and I find new ways to expand my dream and my business every day. Sharing my story and helping others get started are a big part of that. If you're a proud misfit with a creative vision, then this is your book.

XOXO Kingi!!!

1

stuff to get you started

← I ♥ SILKSCREENING:

This print exists because of the book you are reading right now! I was doing the illustrations at the café around the corner from my store, and putting them on the floor to dry as I ran out of room on the table. They looked so cute next to each other down there that I thought I would create a print to celebrate the world of silkscreening equipment. It's amazing that over twenty years of silkscreening, I had never done a print devoted to the actual craft before now!

Welcome

to the ever-growing cult of Peachy Silkscreeners! I have been teaching silkscreen workshops for well over a decade now, in my studio and on the road, and it's still one of my favourite parts of running my own business. Whether I'm teaching college-level fashion design students or eight-year-olds on a craft date with their moms, a private party of beer-drinking bridesmaids who stay till 3AM or my usual Sunday-morning assortment of eclectic, super-keen crafty people, it's always the same: the process of learning and creating draws us together into a printing community, and we begin to support each other's individual ideas and goals. By reading this book, you've become part of that community too. Drop by the store on Queen Street West in Toronto if you're in town, or email us! I love getting messages from students and people who have my how-to DVD, asking technical questions, showing off their new designs, or just saying hi. Celebrate your new status as a silkscreener and don't be shy!

real, no-foolin' do's and don'ts.

Always remember that, as with any membership in a community of equals, responsibilities come with the privileges.

DON'T copy other people's ideas or designs. It's not only an ethical issue, it's your legal responsibility! Make it a priority to research the copyright laws that apply to your work (the information is available on federal government websites). Your strength as an artist will always be your ability to generate your own original ideas.

DO get involved in your local arts scene! No matter where you live, you'll find other like-minded, hardworking artists and crafters who could use your support and encouragement. Attend openings at local galleries, and talk to the artists.

DO participate in local craft shows and sales! You'll build a local, long-term customer base, and you'll meet other crafters. I love to trade at these events.

DO volunteer, or start an initiative of your own. Find out what arts-related organizations need help, or apply your artistic talents to other causes you believe in. A fashion designer friend of mine raised over $20,000 for Hurricane Katrina aid by mobilizing local artists and renting a church basement for a massive sale of crafts and vintage items. She arranged it all in time for the government deadline to match the amount raised!

trash talk!

Don't rule out 'shopping' for trash: you'll be both thrilled and horrified to discover how much, say, usable scrap lumber people throw out! Bathroom renovations can even yield a used tub — OK, it might be avocado with a pattern of rust stains, but it's free, and ideal for studio purposes. Grab a pair of heavy garden gloves to protect your hands, and take a walk around your neighbourhood on the day before large-item garbage pickup. (And you never know what other treasures you might find: a friend of mine, while 'shopping' for a used table, picked up a perfectly good pair of vintage hand-tooled leather boots that needed a $6 repair on one heel.)

need it, got it, need it, built it...

One of the beauties of silkscreening is that you don't need a huge outlay of money or time to get going. Much of the equipment that you do need can be built by your own capable hands, even if you've never built anything before. You don't even need a special studio; when I started out, I did everything from my one-room apartment, with a shared bathroom down the hall!

What you want to know is: what stuff do I need to get started? How much is it going to cost me? Here's a list with **approximate** costs. Don't worry if you've never heard of some of this stuff! The chapters to come have a more detailed breakdown on what you'll need, where to get it, and how to build it...and the rest of the book will teach you how to make it all work! Many of the supplies are available used, whether from online auctions or garage sales, and some things you may already have or can borrow. Your costs will vary depending on how creative you get about saving money.

things you'll need to make a screen and print from it

NOTE: ALL COSTS ARE APPROXIMATE, AND IN CANADIAN DOLLARS!

OBJECT	AVAILABLE USED?	AVAILABLE FREE?	COST IF NEW	NEED IT	GOT IT	MY COST
Tools you'll need in general						
staple gun	Yes	Possibly	$17	☐	☐	_____
hammer	Yes	Possibly	$5	☐	☐	_____
screwdriver	Yes	Possibly	$5	☐	☐	_____
scissors	Yes	Possibly	$5	☐	☐	_____
craft knife	No	Possibly	$4 (knife + blade)	☐	☐	_____
pliers	Yes	Possibly	$5	☐	☐	_____
Screen supplies						
Old pre-made frame	Yes, online auction	Yes, netlists	$10+	☐	☐	_____
OR DIY screen supplies:						
10xx screen mesh	No	No	$25/yd	☐	☐	_____
2 × 2 pine	Yes	Yes, trash!				
stretcher boards	Unlikely	Unlikely	$7/20″ × 24″	☐	☐	_____
wood screws	Yes	Yes	$4/box	☐	☐	_____
mitre board	Possibly	Possibly	$5	☐	☐	_____
staples for gun	No	No	$3/box	☐	☐	_____
carpenter's glue	No	No	$4	☐	☐	_____

OBJECT	AVAILABLE USED?	AVAILABLE FREE?	COST IF NEW	NEED IT	GOT IT	MY COST
Light-exposure supplies:						
Photo emulsion	No	No	$65/gal	☐	☐	_____
			$39/qt	☐	☐	_____
Trough	Unlikely	Unlikely	$45	☐	☐	_____
Board (as screen cover)	Yes	Yes	$5/16″ × 22″	☐	☐	_____
Weights (e.g. cinderblocks)	Yes	Yes	$3	☐	☐	_____
AND (CHOOSE ONE)						
Light table, premade	Yes, online auction	No	$400 at PB	☐	☐	_____
OR DIY Light table supplies:						
24 × 48 fluorescent ceiling light fixture	Yes, online auction	Beware if broken!	$60	☐	☐	_____
Four 48″, 40w UV fluorescent bulbs	No	No	$19 each	☐	☐	_____
24″ × 48″ 5mm piece of glass	No	No	$35	☐	☐	_____
on/off switch	No — new for safety!	No	$3	☐	☐	_____
electrical cord with 3-prong plug	No — new for safety!	No	$5+	☐	☐	_____
OR Lightbulb array exposure supplies:						
Two 60-w light bulbs	Yes	Don't steal 'em!	$10/2 pack	☐	☐	_____
5mm/¼″-thick piece of glass	No	No	$7	☐	☐	_____

OBJECT	AVAILABLE USED?	AVAILABLE FREE?	COST IF NEW	NEED IT	GOT IT	MY COST
Two extension cords with						
lightbulb sockets	Maybe	Maybe	$10	☐	☐	_____
OR Two clip lights	Maybe	Maybe	$12	☐	☐	_____
Wash-out area supplies:						
Length of hose	Yes	Possibly	$ 8	☐	☐	_____
Garden spray-gun	Yes	Yes	$15	☐	☐	_____
OPTIONAL:						
Portable laundry tub	Possibly		$ 25	☐	☐	_____
Used bathtub/laundry tub		Yes	$50	☐	☐	_____
Design supplies:						
india ink	No	No	$ 10/bottle	☐	☐	_____
vellum sheets	No	No	$15/100 pack	☐	☐	_____
acetate	No	No	$7/box	☐	☐	_____
calligraphy pen, nibs	Yes	Possibly	$1–2/ea	☐	☐	_____
paintbrushes	Yes	Yes	$1–2/ea	☐	☐	_____
rubylith/amberlith	No	No	$4.50/sheet	☐	☐	_____
magic tape	No	Possibly	$2/roll	☐	☐	_____
paper	Yes — recycle!	Yes — recycle!	Varies	☐	☐	_____
cardboard	Yes — recycle!	Yes — recycle!	Varies	☐	☐	_____
photocopier	Possibly	Unlikely	$200	☐	☐	_____

OBJECT	AVAILABLE USED?	AVAILABLE FREE?	COST IF NEW	NEED IT	GOT IT	MY COST
Printing surface:						
Ironing board	Yes	Yes, from trash	$20	☐	☐	_____
OR Custom print pad	No	No	$60+ from PB	☐	☐	_____
OR DIY print pad:						
cotton canvas	Yes	Unlikely	$2/yd	☐	☐	_____
carpet underpad	No! It'll be gross!	Ditto	$2/yd	☐	☐	_____
bungee cords	Yes	Yes	$5/package	☐	☐	_____
big safety pins	Yes	Yes	$3/package	☐	☐	_____
OR Print table:						
sturdy table	Yes	Yes	$20 at junk shop	☐	☐	_____
cotton canvas	Yes	Unlikely	$2/yd	☐	☐	_____
carpet underpad	No, it'll be gross	Ditto	$2/yd	☐	☐	_____
thick felt underpad	Unlikely	Unlikely	$75/yd	☐	☐	_____
staples (for gun)	No	No	$ 3/box	☐	☐	_____
Printing sundries:						
packing tape	No	No	$10/3 rolls	☐	☐	_____
nail polish	Yes	Yes — ask friends!	$2	☐	☐	_____
staples	No	Possibly	$3/box	☐	☐	_____
straight pins	Possibly	Possibly	$2/box	☐	☐	_____
squeegee	Possibly	Possibly	$45 wood/15 plastic	☐	☐	_____
paint scraper	Yes	Yes	$2/each	☐	☐	_____

OBJECT	AVAILABLE USED?	AVAILABLE FREE?	COST IF NEW	NEED IT	GOT IT	MY COST
recycled yogurt/ice-cream /takeout containers	Yes		varies by content!	☐	☐	_____
paintbrushes	Yes	Yes	$1–2/ea	☐	☐	_____

Printing inks and pigments:

OBJECT	AVAILABLE USED?	AVAILABLE FREE?	COST IF NEW	NEED IT	GOT IT	MY COST
translucent base	No	No	$15/32 oz	☐	☐	_____
opaque base	No	No	$29/32oz	☐	☐	_____
black pigment	No	No	$10/8oz	☐	☐	_____
coloured pigment	No	No	$10/8oz	☐	☐	_____

Things to print:

OBJECT	AVAILABLE USED?	AVAILABLE FREE?	COST IF NEW	NEED IT	GOT IT	MY COST
Handmade paper	Possibly	Possibly	$2–10/sheet	☐	☐	_____
T-shirts	Yes	Yes	$2 and up	☐	☐	_____
95%+ natural-fibre fabrics	Yes	Yes	$2/yard + up	☐	☐	_____
Garments	Yes	Yes	varies	☐	☐	_____
Bedding	Yes	Yes	varies	☐	☐	_____

Your ideas:

_____

_____

_____

_____

_____

2

creating your
print studio

spray tip!

In our studio wash-out tub, we keep a length of hose attached to the faucet, with an ordinary adjustable spray-gun (the kind you use to water a garden) for maximum screen-cleaning ease. Don't bother with a super high-pressure spray nozzle; it's expensive, and it can damage your screens.

You can take two approaches to what you need in terms of studio real estate: permanent or temporary. If you're lucky enough to own a house, or have some type of permanent access to a basement or laundry room with running water, you can dedicate an area for studio purposes and custom-build equipment to your specifications. But if you live in a rental apartment, or share space with others, you may not have the luxury of leaving your equipment in place. You may even want your silkscreening apparatus to be portable, like I do when I teach out of town.

For a **PERMANENT** studio, you'll need:

A tub or large sink with cold running water to wash out your screens.
The sink should be located in an area that you can mess up with
impunity and leave messed up (like the wash-out area in our
studio). You won't be using anything but water for clean-up, so
you don't require any special ventilation. If you don't have a tub,
you can get one cheaply from a wrecking company, or check on
netlists in your area.

A darkroom, which could be a closet or storage room. Tape a square of
scrap cardboard into the windows if there are any. Weather-strip
the base of the door so that light won't seep in.

A flat print surface at about waist-level. See "Light Carpentry for
Silkscreeners" for all the details on how to build your own print
table, you keener! Costs will vary for lumber and other supplies
depending on the size of table you plan to build — and how much
you can get from the curb on collection day.

Approximate costs for permanent studio real estate:

Used laundry sink/tub	$50
Weatherstripping	$10/kit
Length of hose + spray-gun	$25
Print table	costs vary depending on size

For a TEMPORARY/PORTABLE studio, you'll need:

A tub, large sink or shower enclosure with cold running water. Choose something easy to clean after each use so that you will not inkify and enrage other users. The emulsion and inks we use are water-based, so you won't be requiring toxic (and toxically expensive) solvents for clean-up, or special ventilation.

A closet or bathroom without windows to use as a darkroom. Fit a square of scrap cardboard into the windows if there are any, or drape a coat over them. Plug the base of the door with a rolled-up towel.

A flat print-surface at about waist-level. You can use an ironing board for printing small projects like t-shirts, or make a print pad to cover an existing table. See "Light Carpentry for Silkscreeners" for all the details on how to make one! Costs will vary depending on the size of the pad you want to make, but canvas and carpet underpadding are very cheap. If you prefer, you can use ¾" felt instead of underpadding — it's more expensive, but ultra-durable. We've had the same felt on our print table for over 10 years!

Approximate costs for temporary studio real estate:

Portable plastic washtub (optional!)	$25
Handheld shower attachment	20
Ironing board	$15
OR	
Homemade print pad costs vary with size, but under $20	

shower tip

Got a handheld shower attachment? It's all you need to make your shower a custom wash-out area, complete with curtain to contain the spray-back.

washtub tip

Sometimes, when I teach on the road, my only access to running water is in a public bathroom. The sinks are tiny; where to wash out? I bought a couple of plastic washtubs with collapsible legs at a home supply store. These have a simple drainhole in the middle of the tub, which you position over a toilet. Attach a length of hose (long enough to reach the washtub) to the faucet in the sink, and hey presto! Portable washout area! Believe me, if it works for me on the road, it will work for you in the comfort of your own bathroom.

chicken noodle

GEORGES MOUSTAKI

Gravure

on bubbles!

272

3

where do i get all this stuff?

← TRASHIONISTA:TRASHIONISTA:

I'm a bit of a trashy person! I especially like trashy junk food—the more fake-colored, the better. The "Trashionista" print started with a garbage bag that exploded as I was trying to free it from the big metal trashcan I keep in the kitchen. (See? told you I was trashy!) The garbage made a really interesting pattern on the linoleum. I started rearranging it and adding things, and then I realized it would make a better print than a perishable art installation on my kitchen floor. We like to print this one in thick, bright neon ink on black!

Before you buy, go on a scavenger hunt. You (and/or your roommates, friends and family) probably have a fair number of the items on the list already. What you don't have is probably available from any hardware or home-supply store. The specialized items may require a bit more digging, but it's actually much easier to source suppliers now than when I started my business over two decades ago! And at the risk of sounding infomercial-like, we gals at Peach Berserk are also in the silkscreening supply business, from pre-made light tables and screens to pigments and photo emulsion. Call or email us for a quote, or just for advice.

Silkscreening supply outlets: just do a net search for "silkscreen + supplies" and see what comes up locally or by mail-order.

Art supply stores: good for design supplies, like india ink and rubylith, but beware! Their silkscreen supplies can be very expensive, and the selection is often limited to a few, non-professional-grade items.

Lighting stores: it can be tricky to find a hardware store that carries the 48" UV fluorescent bulbs. If your local one can't order them in for you, your best bet is to approach industrial lighting suppliers (as opposed to places that sell lamps or fixtures).

Hobby/craft outlets: these retailers at your local (gulp) mall probably only carry commercial silkscreening kits, not individual supplies like mesh or emulsion. The kits tend to contain overpriced, cheaply-assembled materials; the premade screen is too tiny to be at all useful; and in my opinion they're just not adequate for serious silkscreeners like you and me!

Netlists and online auctions: especially if you don't live near a large urban centre, online sources can be invaluable. Try locating used materials and equipment; you can get some great deals! As with any online shopping, you need to be informed about what you're looking for and who you're buying from. Do your research: find out the price range for the items you need, and read feedback on the sellers.

on a light-table note...

A light-table is a piece of equipment that silkscreeners use to "shoot" their artwork onto emulsion-coated screens through a few minutes' exposure to ultraviolet light. Although it's essentially just a big, flat lamp with a glass top and special bulbs , the whole idea of a light-table can be daunting to new silkscreeners. For one thing, it's the only item that you need experience to build for yourself, because of the electrical work involved. For another, it's one of the more expensive studio features, whether you build it yourself or not.

If you prefer a non-DIY light-table acquisition plan, you have several options. You could hire someone locally to wire the table for you. It's a simple job for an experienced person; if you provide the materials listed in the "Light Carpentry for Silkscreeners" section, the labour should be an hour or less. Get an entrepreneurial headstart and do a trade for silkscreening services! An electrician might like some T-shirts printed with the company logo, for instance. **Buying a commercially-made table** is a possibility, but make sure it's a light-table designed for exposing silkcreens, not a glorified lightbox for viewing multiple transparencies or slides. It may be listed as an "exposure unit". And beware the price: exposure units can run thousands of dollars, even used. There is absolutely NO reason for you to spend this kind of money! We make and sell our own at Peach Berserk.

You also have the option to **forego the light-table altogether**. You could choose the emulsion-free printing route, and lucky for you, there's a whole section in this book on printing without emulsion and exposure! This is a good alternative if you want to get started right away, or if you need some time to save up for expenses (how cool would it be to fund your light-table with the proceeds from your emulsionless designs?). I've also encountered silkscreeners who successfully **use a non-traditional exposure method** — no, not clothing-optional printing, as much fun as that might be! If you're willing to devote the extra time and material up front for experimentation, and don't mind waiting around for an hour while your screen absorbs enough light to adequately expose the design, it's possible to use an arrangement of plain household lightbulbs. This alternative exposure technique is best for smaller screens, and you won't be able to expose the entire screen surface because of the way the weights must be placed. You'll find the details on what materials you'll need and how to arrange them, at the end of the next chapter. Find out how to use the set-up in Chapter 7, "Fire When Ready: Shooting Your Design Onto The Screen."

silkscreener's shopping list!

I ALREADY HAVE	I'M GETTING FOR FREE	I HAVE TO BUY	I WANT TO BUILD	WISH LIST

4

light carpentry for silkscreeners

Darin' Damzels happened because I was hanging out at a cottage north of Toronto. As soon as I woke up surrounded by trees, I couldn't stop drawing naked women. The curlicues of them reminds me of the long sinuous lines and knots in woodgrain. The more I drew the ladies, the more ladies there were to draw! My friends got really mad at me because they wanted us to go outside and do nature stuff, but all I could do was work on my print.

things you will need:

waterproof glue

staple gun (and staples)

When I first started out, I didn't have the money to buy pre-made items like screens (even if I could find a source for them back then!). I learned to make things myself, and DIY is still a big part of the Peach Berserk philosophy. Why buy it when you can make it to fit, and do it on the cheap? Check our handy table in Chapter 1 for approximate price ranges.

making a silkscreen frame

There are a couple of ways to approach screen building.

Art supply stores carry painting stretcher frames in a variety of lengths. ① These grooved pine pieces have mitred corners, so you can just ② slip them together into a neat frame, and secure the corners with your trusty staple-gun, and/or some carpenter's glue. So easy! Screen frames made from stretchers are less durable than ones made from scratch, though, and you are limited by the size of the pre-cut lengths.

things you will need:

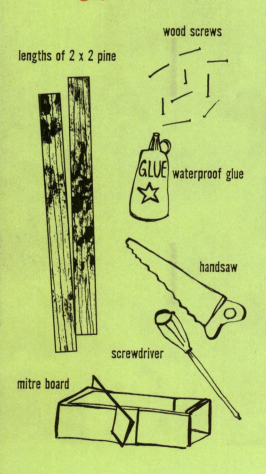

lengths of 2 x 2 pine

wood screws

GLUE waterproof glue

handsaw

screwdriver

mitre board

1

I made my own screens when I was starting out, but now the studio is so busy that I get someone handy to make them for me. A person with carpentry skills can get a lot of these done in a very short time, so it's an inexpensive job to outsource if you don't want to make your own.

Recycle or buy pieces of 2 × 2 lumber. Pine is best because it's light and easy to handle, dries quickly, and doesn't warp.

We make screens in two sizes: the small is 20″ × 25″ and the large is 33″ × 48″. We don't make them any larger because they get too unwieldy and difficult to

handle and wash! The big ones suit repeating-pattern prints or large-format images, and the small ones are great for t-shirts or single images.

① Cut the edges of the wood on an angle, using the 45-degree setting on the mitre board as a guide.

② Glue and screw the sides together.

things you will need:

sturdy wooden table

carpet underpadding or ¾" felt

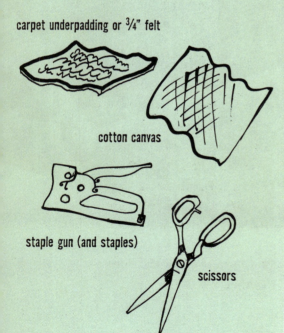

cotton canvas

staple gun (and staples)

scissors

making a permanent tabletop print surface
(best for permanent studio space)

There's much less to making a print table than meets the eye! If you're feeling adventurous and have access to a lot of lumber, you can custom-build a table to your own specifications. For instance, in my studio, I wanted to use the space under the print table for screen storage, so the height of the biggest screen determined the height of the table. The length of the studio itself was the only limit to the table's length! For me, a custom table was the perfect solution to meet the needs of my business. I even built a second one upstairs when the under-the-table storage got too crowded.

You may find it cheaper and less hassle to recycle an old but still sturdy table (again, check the neighbourhood curbs on collection day if you don't have one knocking around). Lean over the top surface and see if you feel comfortable working at this height. If not, raise the table up by nailing chunks of scrap wood to its feet, or place it on a support of bricks or cinderblock. Just make sure it's stable, and will stay that way while you're slapping screens down on it.

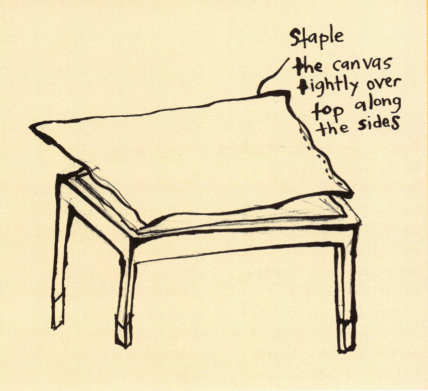

Staple the canvas tightly over top along the sides

felt or underpad— what's under your canvas?

For an ultra–durable print table, felt can't be beat. We've never had to replace the felt on our studio print table, although we print on it all day, every day, and the canvas gets replaced every other month. It's a good thing, since the initial investment was substantial. Felt is pretty much bulletproof, but it's very expensive. It's best for permanent installations, or for a temporary pad that you plan to drag everywhere with you on a regular basis! If you're short of funds, or you don't think you'll be punishing your print surface through heavy use and/or travel, carpet underpadding is MUCH cheaper and it's easily sourced.

Buy a piece of ¾″-thick felt, or carpet underpadding at least 1″ thick, to cover the table surface, leaving a gap of about 15″ all around.

Centre the padding on the table, then cover the whole tabletop with canvas and staple it taut to the wooden area surrounding the padding. Don't staple *through* the padding; it will wear away at the attachment points. Use the longest staples that will fit in your gun (we like JT21 5⁄16″ / 8mm for this job), or else use nails.

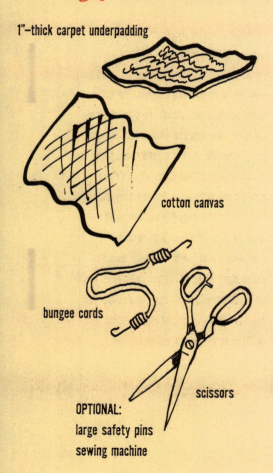

things you will need:

1"-thick carpet underpadding

cotton canvas

bungee cords

scissors

OPTIONAL:
large safety pins
sewing machine

making a portable print pad
(best for temporary studio space)

Say you don't feel like making a whole print table, or you want a print surface you can roll up and store when you're not using it. You can make a canvas 'pillowcase' that enfolds a piece of underpadding, and bungee it to any table surface. I travel with a few of these when I teach in other cities; mine have buttonholes around the edges that the bungees hook into, but plain old holes in the canvas will work just as well. You can edge the holes with duct tape to prevent fraying (and for DIY street cred).

Measure the tabletop you plan to use most as a print surface. You want your print pad to fit within these measurements. Trim the carpet underpadding to size, and cut out a piece of canvas that will fold over it, covering it on both sides with about 3" extra all around.

Use a sewing machine to sew through the canvas all around the underpadding, sealing it in. Don't sew through the underpadding! It's no problem if the seams aren't right up against the edge of the padding; when the bungee cords are in place, you'll still get a tight, smooth

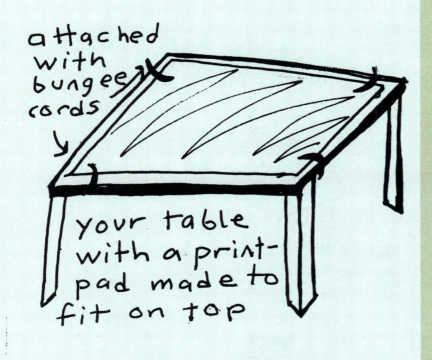

attached with bungee cords →

your table with a print-pad made to fit on top

surface. If you don't have access to a sewing machine, you can just pin the canvas together at 2″ intervals with large-size safety pins (and you'll have an even tougher DIY look, especially combined with the duct-taped holes).

Now, make an even number of holes on either side of the pad, keeping closer to the underpadding than to the edge of the canvas. You'll hook a bungee into one hole, stretch it beneath the table, and hook the other end into the opposite hole. Larger pads will require more holes, but any size pad should have at least two bungees holding it in place for printing.

things you will need:

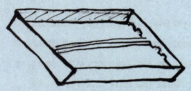

One 24 x 48" fluorescent ceiling-light fixture
(available at hardware stores
or big-box building supply outlets)

One 24 x 48" piece of 5mm/$\frac{1}{4}$" glass (ask the
glass supplier to sand the edges for you after
cutting; they are extremely sharp)

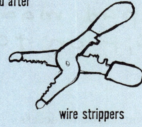

wire strippers

side cutters

pliers

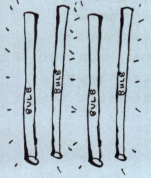

Four 48" long, 40-watt
uv fluorescent bulbs
(ultra-violet), model
code f40/350bl

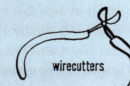

electrical tape and wire caps

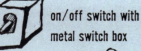

on/off switch with
metal switch box

wirecutters

length of electrical cord with 3-prong plug

2 self-threading metal screws

multihead screwdriver

making a light table

IMPORTANT SAFETY NOTE: you **must** have experience with electrical work for this project. If you're not, follow the instructions below ONLY under proper supervision by a person with electrical training and experience.

Remove the plastic light-diffusing screen from the fixture (that's the knobbly translucent sheet hiding the bulbs). Find some creative use for it elsewhere, because you won't be needing it again for this project.

Open the access trough of the lamp and feed the main power line out the side.

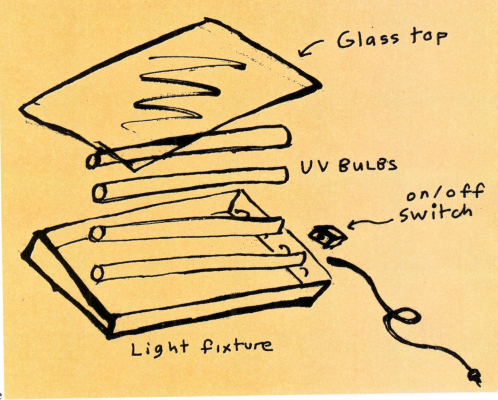

Glass top

UV BULBS

on/off switch

Light fixture

Attach switch box to side and feed the cables through.
Wire the switch into the power line, and attach the extension with the three-prong plug into the incoming side as per electrical standards.

Put a cap on the switch box.

Fit the 4 bulbs into the casing.

Carefully slide the glass cover into place.

Plug in. Let there be ultraviolet light!

things you will need:

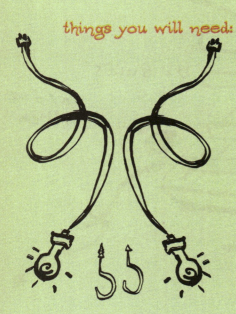

Any table surface that will accommodate your screen

Two extension cords with lightbulb sockets + cup hooks to hang them from

OR Two clip lights

Two heavy weights, such as cinderblocks

Two 60-watt light bulbs (energy-saving ones work well)

One piece of 5mm / ¼"-thick glass, big enough to cover your screen (ask the glass supplier to sand the edges for you after cutting; they are extremely sharp)

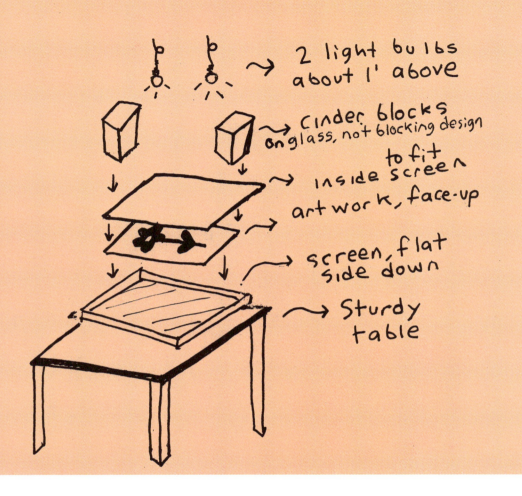

2 light bulbs about 1' above

cinder blocks on glass, not blocking design

inside screen to fit

artwork, face-up

screen, flat side down

sturdy table

arranging your alternative exposure unit
(no light table involved!)

Suspend the two extension cords so that the lightbulbs hang about 15″ above the surface of the table. Cuphooks are ideal because you can just screw them into the ceiling, but if holes in the paintwork mean that you'll lose your security deposit, use clip lights!

That's all you need to do to set up! Directions for using this alternative exposure method are in Chapter 7, "Fire When Ready"

rules
for screen prep:
screen prep rules!

← I HAVEN'T GOT A THING TO WEAR:

I was getting ready for a date one night and looking through my wardrobe, and it struck me! All day I had been designing a print with different dress styles, but it wasn't really working. Then I thought of drawing little hangers for the dresses, and that idea pulled this print together for me. I was so excited about the breakthrough that I cancelled my date, stayed home and sat on the floor in front of the tv, finishing my print! There's still a strong demand for it even though it was one of my first. Of all my designs, this is one that I feel really works, graphically and as an expression of what Peach Berserk is all about, and one that seems to have a special meaning for my customers. People tell me their stories: how they bought something at Peach Berserk when they were 14 and it inspired them to be creative, or how a custom prom dress made their daughter feel like a princess. It's the high point of my day when I get a photo of someone wearing my designs to their wedding, or on their travels to somewhere I may never go. Then I add it to my collection on the change-room walls at Peach Berserk!

rule for stretching

Pull as hard as you can when stretching mesh! In fact, pull harder than you can, then pull some more!

rule for stapling

Shoot the staples on a diagonal to the straight edges of the frame. They hold better than when placed perpendicular or parallel to the edge.

get your mesh on!
stretching your screen

Your wooden frame, made according to the directions in "Light Carpentry for Silkscreeners", is now ready for the next phase of its life as a silkscreen.

You're going to stretch that beautiful 10xx white mesh you bought over the frame to prepare it for printing. Stretch the mesh as tight as you can get it; you want to be able to tap on it like a drum when you're done, or bounce a quarter off it. Emulsion coats a tight screen better, and that means a clearer image and greater ease of printing. Repeat the mantra: **Tighter is righter! Floppy is sloppy!**

things you will need:

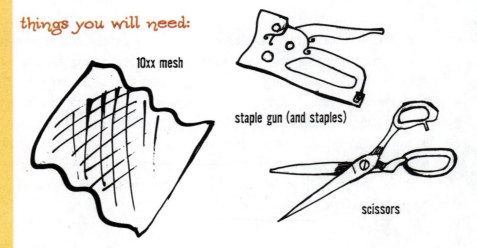

10xx mesh

staple gun (and staples)

scissors

1 "Clip and rip" a piece of mesh big enough to cover your frame with about two inches extra all around. Here's how to do it: Make a tiny "clip" with scissors at the edge of your mesh, and just rip off a piece. Be sure to tear with the grain of the fabric; it's the way the fabric "wants" to tear, and it results in a straight torn edge without the need of measuring or scissors. Now clip and rip two strips of mesh about ¾″ wide. (You'll use them to reinforce your screen as you stretch it.)

Fold the mesh over itself by about ¾″ on two adjacent sides of the frame, and staple a couple of times in the corner where the sides meet.

2 Stretch and staple one of the resultant free-flapping ends.

3 Starting in the middle of the frame, staple to each end, placing staples on the diagonal about ½″ apart. Repeat for the opposite corner. Your extra mesh should hang out about 2″ on the unstapled sides. These are the sides that require the reinforcement strips.

Grab the mesh and pull it to the corner diagonally opposite the one you first stapled. Staple down when you can't take the pulling any more.

rules for screen prep ✳ 49

short on mesh, long on scraps?

Mesh is just a specialized type of fabric, and like any fabric, it can be sewn! If you have mesh ends that aren't quite big enough to cover a screen, don't despair. Sew them together and make a patchwork screen. It will work just as well as a regular one — as long as there's no seam where the print goes! For instance, you can sew right down the middle and place two images on the screen, one on either side of the seam. Don't have enough mesh for reinforcing strips? No problem. Just use a length of ribbon, or tear a strip off any scrap piece of fabric.

4 For each side, staple a strip in the corner and stretch to the other side. Staple down the opposite end. Now, pull the screen mesh tight under the strip, starting from the middle of the frame, and staple down as you go. Repeat for other side.

Trim off excess mesh and hammer down any staples that may still be sticking up.

5 Now you have a gorgeous screen! It was tough, but it was worth it! And you're going to love the next step: you get to slop emulsion on it now. "Was it for *this* I did all that pulling?!"

can you ever be too even or too thin (if you're emulsion)?
how to coat your screen.

1 We use a trough to coat the screens with photo emulsion. You don't need much emulsion per screen, but don't be too stingy either — emulsion, like supermodels, *can* be too thin. If you don't apply enough, it won't expose properly and you'll get tiny open areas of mesh where you don't want them. If you apply emulsion too thickly, it takes longer to shoot, and you risk underexposing the screen. Don't stress, though! You'll find that preparing and shooting screens is more of an art than a science; there's a lot of trial and error involved, and you develop a feel for what's right after a lot of practice. The main thing is to apply smoothly and evenly, and press hard! Don't be chicken that you'll rip the mesh; you should hear a scraping sound.

things you will need:

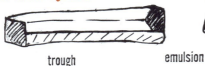

trough   emulsion

New emulsion needs to be sensitized before use. Be sure to check your emulsion's packaging for directions peculiar to the brand. Fill the sensitizer bottle that comes with the emulsion three-quarters full with cold or lukewarm water — NOT hot! Shake until the contents are completely dissolved, then pour all that liquid into the emulsion and mix until you achieve a uniform colour. Your emulsion is now sensitized and ready to use. Always keep the lid on it, and store it in a cool place. If the weather's hot and steamy where you live, you can refrigerate sensitized emulsion, but make sure to label it boldly and clearly so that no-one mistakes it for an edible substance — no joke.

② You coat a screen in four directions: on one side of the screen, start by applying bottom-to-top, then side-to-side. Now flip the screen over and repeat for the other side. It's okay if the bands of emulsion overlap a little bit, but avoid going right to the edge of the screen. It's best not to apply any emulsion within 1″ of the sides.

③ Now use the trough to scrape off excess emulsion: bottom to top on the front of the screen, and then side-to-side on the opposite side. Tilt the trough back slightly to guard against reapplying emulsion while you scrape! The ideal coating is EVEN and THIN. Return the excess emulsion you collect to its container for re-use on another screen. Emulsion won't come off if you let it dry on your trough, so wash that trough immediately after use.

4 When you're sure the coating is as thin and even as you can make it, put the screen in your darkroom to cure until dry. It takes about one hour; you'll know it's dry when it's no longer tacky to the touch. If you have a silkscreening super-emergency and you simply can't wait an hour, do what we do and get in that darkroom with a hairdryer!

Emulsion won't dry properly below room temperature; don't dry your screen in a chilly room.

don't expose yourself (if you're a screen) (or even if you're not).

If you forget about your coated screen and leave it in the darkroom for over two weeks, it will expose itself over time, and be forever ruined for silkscreening purposes. You'll have to tear off the mesh and start again, and that would be tragic for everyone concerned.

feel like stripping?

Maybe, but when it comes to your screen, don't take it all off. Screen-stripper is a solvent that removes exposed emulsion from your screen. We don't use it for a number of reasons: first of all, we shoot our screens carefully, so we won't have to re-do them! Screen-stripper is also toxic, ecologically unfriendly, and I've never seen it work well enough to justify its use.

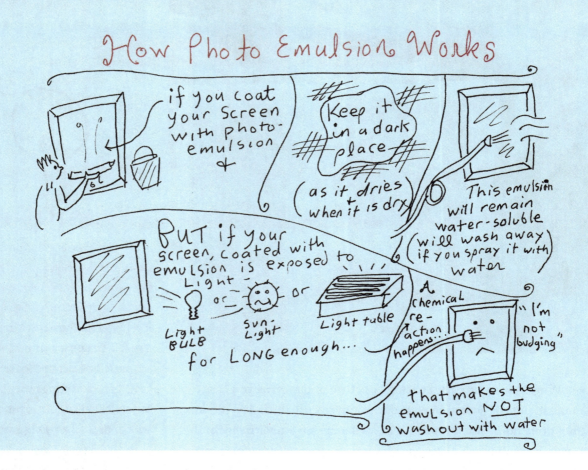

while you're waiting for the screen to dry, let's explore why you just did what you did.

The photo emulsion, when dry, is light-sensitive and water-soluble. If you don't expose it to light, the emulsion can be washed off the screen with water. If you *do* expose it to light for long enough, it does not wash out with water — it becomes a permanent part of the screen. The design you are going to shoot onto your screen will be opaque on a translucent background; that means the emulsion under the design remains unexposed to light. (We'll discuss how to prepare your design for shooting in chapter 7, "You're Blocking My Light: Designing Your Opaque Print").

So, you are going to BLOCK the light where you want the emulsion to wash away (in the shape of your design) when you expose your screen to Light.

For example,.... you want to make a print of Stars

① ✂ ☆ ☆ ↙ ← Cut some star shapes out of a piece of cardboard. (cardboard is opaque + will block the Light, right?)

② Expose your screen (that has been coated with emulsion + left to dry in a dark place). ← board
your screen
opaque art work
Light table

③ wash-out unexposed emulsion
← the emulsion will wash away whereever the cardboard blocked the Light

④ Once your screen is dry... ✓ your fabric ↘
Squish ink thru the screen (it will squish thru where your design is) + PRINT PRINT PRINTS
ink

To shoot your screen, you prepare a giant silkscreen sandwich: light table at the bottom; next layer, opaque design; then the screen with dry emulsion; then a board; and finally weights (like cinder blocks or bricks). Basically, you block the light to your screen wherever your print is, so that the rest of the emulsion will become permanently sealed around it. Where your print is, the emulsion is unexposed, so it's still water-soluble. You can wash it out, leaving open mesh that you squish the ink through to make your print!

6

throwing the perfect print party

design basics for silkscreeners

FASHION PLATE:← FASHION PLATE:

I was wandering around New York City, windowshopping, and I happened to see cute plates in a window display. I started thinking about the lost art of dinner: matching china, complicated recipes, the right forks and the right wine. I imagined those cute dishes, loaded down with the kind of food I never make, printed onto dresses that someone might wear to a dinner party, and "Fashion Plate" was born. This print isn't about the the way I eat at all—I never have gravy in a gravy boat—but I love the way it evokes the essential pleasure of sitting down to dinner. I knew right away that pen and ink would be ideal for drawing the dinner plates freehand, and connecting them with curves and ornamental lines.

What makes a truly outstanding print? Let's put it this way. Have you ever been to a really great party, where the ambiance is perfect, they play all the tunes you love, there's a bevy of bevvies, yummy food, and everyone you talk to is interesting and/or hot? All the elements seem to harmonize and flow together as single entity, The Party, and it just gets better as the night progresses. The same things that make a great party also make a great print.

Imagine you're the host of your print party.

Invite a mix of people. You know how work parties are almost invariably a drag? You know everyone there, you talk shop all night, and you know exactly what to expect, right down to that guy from accounting getting drunk and trying to lure you into the photocopy room. A party gets going when people with different backgrounds and interests start finding connections amongst themselves. It's the same with your print: combining a variety of elements — like lines, curves, areas of light and dark, or different colours — will make your design exciting. But don't lose sight of the ultimate goal — the harmony of the party is sacrificed if the guests just draw attention to themselves and don't find ways to interact.

Rhythm in design results from repeating patterns or lines. Too much repetition can be boring: you wouldn't just play the same song over and over at exactly the same interval all night, but you might mix it with another song, change the volume, sample it, or play it at different times. Think about the mood you want your print to create. Repeating curves and long, flowing lines, like the ones I use in my Matisse-inspired "Life is Beautiful" print, give a restful, contemplative feeling. Changing the size of a repeated form, or randomly distributing it, can shake up the viewers and keep their eyes moving around the print.

Get the lighting right. Too bright, and it feels like a group therapy meeting in a prison. Too dark, and people can't find their way to the bar. Your party needs carefully-planned areas of light and dark that convey a mood and don't overwhelm each other or the guests. So does your print. The light comes from *negative space* — basically, the unprinted areas of your design — and conversely, the dark is supplied by the printed parts. This applies even if you're printing white-on-white! Sometimes, your goal is to highlight the contrast between light and dark (leaving the overhead light on in the bathroom so your guests can see it from down the hall); other times, you want a subtle interplay (like candles scattered all around the living room). The negative space plays just as important a role in your design as the printed area. Placing contrasting elements close together emphasizes their difference.

Where's the bar? Did you check out the buffet? Every party has a focal point, the place everyone wants to get to and revisit all night. In a print, the place your eye is drawn to right away is the dominant element. If you have too many dominant elements, they compete with each other for the viewer's attention. You don't know where to look first: it's like walking into a room with three bars and two live bands and a burlesque performer and a demonstration of glassblowing techniques. Remember that the dominant element doesn't have to be smack in the middle, unless you want it to be.

Decide on standing room only, languid lounging, or a mix. If everyone's standing up, the party has more movement than if you provide comfy chaise-longues for everyone. Horizontal forms and lines in your print will lend a sense of restfulness and peace; vertical and diagonal ones encourage the viewer's gaze to move from place to place within the design. (A wardrobe note: it's a fashion myth that vertical stripes make you look tall and skinny. In fact, they encourage the eye to trace the contours of any curves they cover.)

Keep everything in proportion. Inviting only the loudmouths you know would be just as disastrous for conversation as inviting only the painfully shy. But maybe you don't want everyone to be sharing in the discussion equally; maybe your party has a guest of honour whom you want everyone to meet, or a performance that calls for silence from the attendees. Maintaining balance in your print can go beyond a simple half-this, half-that equilibrium — there's literally a Golden Rule (or Mean) for achieving proportion that pleases the eye, and it dates back to ancient Greece. When you are using two forms or lines together, the smaller one should relate to the larger as the larger relates to the whole.

It's over when it's over. At the end of the perfect party, when there's nothing left but tomorrow's dishes and some melted ice in the bathtub, you don't beg everyone to stay for just another hour, or run out into the street to drag in someone, *anyone*, to keep it going. You wave goodbye to your guests and fall asleep planning your next triumph. When you're designing, it can be difficult to know how much is too much (even when "too much" is what you're going for). Learn to trust your instincts; if you have a gut feeling that a design is finished, it probably is. Tack your design to the wall and see how it looks from across the room. Step away, even for an hour or so, and look at it afresh before you decide to add that extra element — at least in a permanent form.

Remember everything the next day. The hostess-etiquette guides used to recommend that you keep a record of your events, including who was invited to what occasion, what food and wine was served, etc. That way, you could avoid mistakes (like duplicating a dish that flopped the first time) while building your reputation as an imaginative and thoughtful entertainer. Keeping a scrapbook-style printmaker's journal will help you remember what worked and what didn't, as well as providing a place to put all those inspirational bits and pieces you find.

7

you're blocking my light

designing your opaque print

← VOODOO LADY:

I designed "Voodoo Lady" back at the turn of the millenium, because I wanted to contrast girliness with a skull-and-crossbones graphic: kind of like wearing biker boots with a party dress. There was a lot of upheaval in my life at the time. I was newly divorced with a nine-month-old baby, and I felt like exploring my darker, edgier side while expressing the crazy freedom change can bring. So I got a tattoo of an anchor that says "Dad" underneath it, and I drew lots of fairly non-threatening skulls while sitting in bed at 3:00am, breastfeeding my daughter. "VooDoo Lady" was an instant favourite with staff and customers. I've made lots of wedding dresses in it, especially in pink and lime green, or silver and black. Now, of course, skulls are mainstream, even in catalogue stuff and kidswear. But that's fashion for you.

first, the background information

You can create all kinds of opaque design with any number of media, but for silkscreening, the background is always the same: light must be able to pass through it! For a translucent background, I use acetate or vellum, or I just place an object onto the light-table glass and let nothingness be the background (good for nihilists). Vellum is preferable to acetate because photocopy or printer toner adheres better and makes the image more opaque. You have to print (or copy) your image onto two sheets of acetate and layer them to get the same opacity as a single print on vellum — and in the long run that makes vellum the cheaper option, too. To keep your costs down even further, buy your vellum in rolls from an art supply store. You can draw or write on the vellum (unlike acetate), either directly off the roll for large designs, or cut your own printer-size sheets. Vellum even cuts more easily than acetate. If the thought of all that measuring and cutting makes you crazy, don't worry: vellum is also available in lettersize sheets.

berserk-tested methods of print design

There are so many different ways to design an opaque print for exposure and printing. Here are some of the methods and media I use to create the designs for our expanding library of prints. I'm constantly experimenting with new ones, and revisiting the old ones with a fresh twist of Peach. Use these ideas on their own or in combination with one or more of the others. Even if you have an attention deficit like me, I guarantee you'll never get tired of opaque print design; there's always something new to try, and trying it leads to even more ideas and techniques.

When I'm thinking about a new print, I like to choose my design medium by visualizing the finished product that will showcase it — let's say, a skirt printed with flowers. Say I want it to look like I *painted* the flowers all over the fabric; then I'd use a brush and india ink. If I want a sketched, flowing look, as if a renaissance artist drew the flowers, I make the artwork with charcoal. If I'm envisioning a mod mini, I might use high-contrast photographic images of flowers for my print.

Determining the mood of your design is a great way to figure out the art supplies you are going to need. Here's a list of my Moody Media; there's space for you to start your own at the end of the chapter!

india ink
organic, expressive, old-fashioned

India ink is one of my favourites, and you can buy it by the bottle at any art supply store.

Why am I in love with it? Because it's inexpensive; it's opaque by nature, especially when applied thickly (so your design doesn't need to be photocopied before you can shoot it); and a bottle lasts forever, even if you spill it now and then!

Use india ink in three basic ways:

1 Pen and nib.

Get a least one pen (nib holder) and a few different nib sizes and shapes to fit into it. Sharp nibs will give you finer lines, but don't go *too* fine: very fine lines are hard to expose properly onto your screen, and don't print well because of the thickness of textile printing ink and the texture of fabric. Also, play around with different shapes of nibs; round, square, or pointed will all give a different look to your design.

Pen and ink gives you the freedom to vary the thickness of the line through the pressure you put on the pen, the amount of ink in the nib, and even the way you rotate the pen as you draw. Experiment!

You achieve a very organic, old-fashioned expressive line to your drawing. Often when I draw with pen and ink, ink sprays off the pen, leaving a jumble of dots of the page. I don't let that bother me. I think it adds to the design!

2 Brush.

If you are looking for a very expressive, romantic, painterly look to your print, a brush with india ink is perfect. As with nibs, I like to have a variety of brushes. The cheap, hard-bristle ones are best, in all different thicknesses. Sometimes I get extra creative, and I cut my brushes off at an angle with scissors for an interesting line as I paint.

3 Stamps.

You can have a lot of fun with stamp style prints. There's no limit to stampable items: whatever will hold still long enough to be inked and printed. Try your hands and feet, or your kids'; flat flowers (like daisies); even pretend you're back in grade 3, cut up fruits and veggies and use those! You will probably still need to photocopy the resultant stamped image to make it even more opaque, since coverage may be thin in some areas, and you will lose that detail when you shoot.

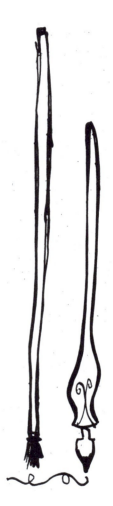

markers
industrial, modern, clean

Whatever you draw with a marker, whether a thick one or a fine-point, can be made into a print. The same rule applies for markers as for pen nibs — don't go too fine, or the line won't shoot or print properly. Markers give your print a VERY different mood than pen and ink do — industrial, pop-art, modern, disposable, are all associations that come to mind for me.

There are two ways you can work with markers.

1 Use opaque markers, draw directly on vellum, and expose onto your screen.

2 Use regular markers, draw onto regular paper, and when your design is done, photocopy it onto vellum and expose onto your screen.

I prefer the second option, because opaque markers are expensive, hard to find, don't come in many thicknesses (or point shapes) and dry out quickly. Also, I would rather mess around with cheap markers on cheap paper, try tons of stuff, and *then* when I get the design just right, photocopy it on to vellum!

charcoal, crayon
grainy, freeform, spontaneous

Charcoal reminds me of my old art school days. It suits screen printing really well, because it makes very grainy, expressive lines. For best results, draw in quick, spontaneous, free-form strokes, with charcoal dust flying everywhere! Press really hard for very black sharp lines, and then ease up for lots of crazy shading. You will feel like a serious artist, but as soon as your masterpiece is done, photocopy it onto vellum before it smudges or too much of the dark areas get knocked off through handling (spraying it with fixative is also an option).

You can never outgrow **crayons**, although I do love giving them to kids and making their drawings into prints. It's great to have children drawing around you anyway; they draw so freely and for fun, and are happy with their own crazy interpretation of things. We can all learn from that! Crayon makes distinctively textured lines and areas of shading, and like charcoal, needs to be photocopied onto vellum to make it opaque.

other drawing media
eccentric, edgy

The obvious choice for a graffiti-inspired print, spray paint is fun to use and gives an urban look. I once drew a print all in lipstick! Keep experimenting; you never know what might work, and what *doesn't* work can be even more instructive. Whatever you use, assume that it's probably not opaque enough for shooting onto a screen. When in doubt, photocopy onto vellum.

cardboard
chunky, funky, childlike

Cardboard is a must for us print designers. It blocks light perfectly, and everyone has some hanging around their house, so it's free! Just grab a pair of scissors and cut out chunky shapes — the art of Matisse is a great inspiration for this. Ripping the cardboard creates interesting edges. Since they're opaque, you can lay the pieces directly onto your screen, or arrange and photocopy them onto vellum if you want to preserve the exact design for eventual re-shooting.

" really, this is cardboard"

rubylith/amberlith
fluid, curvy, precise and finely detailed

Does Rubylith here? Does Amberlith with her? Rubylith is a layer of red, light-impermeable, gel-like material layered onto sheets of acetate (amberlith is the same thing, just a different colour). It was indispensible to the pre-digital lithography industry, but it's still widely used in craft applications, and you can buy it in large sheets at art supply stores. Rubylith is transparent, so you can place it over the image you want to cut out and trace shapes with a craft knife, peeling away and discarding the thin layer of red from the acetate beneath as you go. Make sure you connect your cut lines so that the red layer can peel away smoothly without ripping. Use a light touch with the knife: you don't want to cut through the acetate, or your design will fall apart. The clear areas will stay "clear" of ink in the resultant print; wherever the red remains will print.

To me, rubylith is *the* miracle material. When you cut a line with a craft blade, it feels like the rubylith is the ice and you're figure-skating your design. It's magic how smooth, fluid curves and intricate details flow from the sharpness and precision of a blade slicing into the ruby.

1 Complex cut-out designs. Rubylith is good for the designs that it would drive you crazy to cut out of cardboard.

2 Tracing found images, like photographs. Leave the dark, or shadowed, areas of the picture red, and peel away the rest. This works especially well with high-contrast photographs of faces, as in our example.

3 Curvy silhouettes. I have a print of curvy women's silhouettes, and rubylith suited them perfectly.

4 Pop or mod art designs, like big flowers or designs based on 50s/60s abstract art.

5 Spot colour in a line-drawing print. Spot colour means adding a second colour (or third, or fourth…) to a line-drawing print, and it can bring depth and dimension to your design. As with our example here, I think spot colour works best if it doesn't fit exactly inside the lines of your drawing, but just adds an extra blob of colour! It's easier to print, too, because you don't have to worry about precision printing, and you get a interesting negative space between the drawing and the rubylith colour.

6 Spot colour in a photographic print. Andy Warhol is patron saint of this technique; apply to him for inspiration! Just put your piece of rubylith on top of the photograph you are going to use, and leave red areas where you want to add colour. Simple! Add eyeshadow (extra effective if it is a photo of an ex-dictator). Add lipstick, a hair colour, whatever!

7 Custom type design. A lot of people get stuck thinking that the only lettering you are 'allowed' to use comes from computer fonts or books — no way! Rubylith is ideal for cutting out your own style of type, and the zanier the better, in my book!

get rid of that grey (if you're a photograph):

PREPARING YOUR PHOTO IMAGE FOR MAXIMUM PRINTABILITY

Any photo image, black-and-white or colour, will need to be made high-contrast in order to strip away the grey tones that would muddy your final print. **This rule applies to colour drawings as well!** You can run your images through a high-contrast filter on your computer, or go low-tech and photocopy it repeatedly. Keep this in mind when you select your initial image: a full-length wedding photo against a mid-toned background will be much harder to reproduce as a print than a close-up of the couple. By the time you've reduced the grey in the first example, you'll have lost all the detail from the faces. Find images that have strong contrast to begin with.

how to make a cool colour print from a photograph

select your image, and photocopy it lighter to get rid of grey tones; then photocopy the resulting image darker. Copy the now high-contrast photo onto vellum. You can do a second colour in rubylith.

photocopy objects
witty, humourous, ironic

Scissors, forks, nails... I photocopied a real banana once and used my miracle substance (say it with me now!) rubylith, to add a second colour. Plaid fabric, or lace, makes a great print — just enlarge it before you photocopy it onto vellum. Some objects don't provide enough contrast in their natural state; you will have to spray paint them black before photocopying.

found images
disposable, transient, topical

Once you start looking, you'll find them everywhere. They will follow you home. I assigned a group of co-op students to collect stuff about our neighbourhood (Queen and Bathurst) within a three-block radius of the store, and we collaged it all and printed it! What about historic symbols? Antique magazine advertisements? Classified ads can be used in their original state or retouched for editorial commentary. Even old weird plaques can work: our "Which Miss Are You?" print was inspired by a particularly bizarre garage-sale find, which now hangs on my lime-green kitchen wall. Don't forget that you can shoot found objects **directly** onto your screen, too. We've done this with leaves and wire coathangers. Just find something flat that you can tape directly on your screen and shoot!

Frederick Noel Carpenter circa 1930's.

don't leave inspiration off your shopping list!

You've probably got lots of design ideas already, but inspiration keeps them coming and you can never have enough! Observe the world around you all the time. Travel is my absolute fave, number–one way to get inspired, but even if I can't get away, I love going to my hometown art galleries, or going window–shopping for high fashion. I daydream all the time; many of my designs are based on my idea of a perfect fantasy world.

photographs
journalistic, retro, personal, political

Prints based on family photographs make great presents, and wouldn't you know, old black-and-white photos tend to have the high contrast that makes them perfect for silkscreening! Images of people or places in the news can help make political statement, and old found photos from catalogues or magazines create a retro look. Use the photos alone or in a repeated-image print, or add other media to existing images. I like to caption 1950s fashion catalogue images with speech bubbles in india ink; our Lady Libbers I and II prints are best-selling examples.

typefaces and print
conversational, provocative

Manipulate handwriting or found lettering by enlarging it and repeatedly photocopying. An old letter, alone or overlaid with images, could make a bittersweet memorial to lost love. You can try massaging a favourite typeface into a new and original form on your computer. Consider silkscreening the invitations to your next major event — text and all!

moody media shopping list

ITEM	MOOD
India Ink	_____
	_____
Markers	_____
	_____
Charcoal	_____
	_____
Other drawing stuff	_____
	_____
Cardboard	_____
	_____
Rubylith/Amberlith	_____
	_____
Found images	_____
	_____
Photocopied objects	_____
	_____
Photographs	_____
	_____
Found shapes	_____
	_____
Typefaces	_____
	_____

fire when ready
shooting your design onto the screen

← **I LOVE A MAN IN UNIFORM:**

This print takes a page from my dad's life: the 1937 yearbook showing his graduating class in military school. I enlarged the pictures, and the more grainy they looked, the more I liked them. I wanted an extreme vintage look as well as very clear contrast between the areas of light and dark. Using family photographs for printing lets you keep a part of your personal history alive through your art. When people ask about this print in the store, I get to talk about my dad, his life and accomplishments. I'm proud of my dad, and I'm proud of this print too.

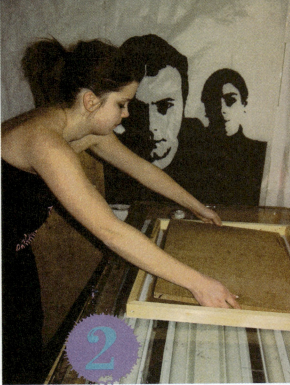

Your designs are satisfactory in every detail and camera-ready: rendered opaque on vellum. Your ultra-taut, emulsion-coated screen has spent an hour or so in the darkroom. You are ready to take the first step in shooting your screen.

exposure using a light-table

① Flip your design over so that the back side is facing up. The image should be opposite to the way you want it to print; for instance, if you have text, you should not be able to read the words (unless you're Leonardo Da Vinci and do all your writing backwards). Now place the image(s) on the top side of the screen — the side that is "flat", flush with the wooden frame. You can place more than one image on the screen for shooting, but leave a margin of an inch or two all around each one. Keep your images away from the edges of the screen; the area closest to the frame is invariably the least evenly-coated with emulsion. Tape each image

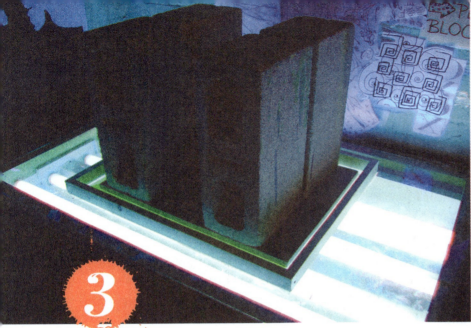

3

4

down securely on the screen with ordinary adhesive tape (we like the matte-finish kind).

Flip the screen over and ensure that no images are overlapping or folded over.

Place the screen on the light table glass, flat side down.

2 Place your board on top of the screen. The board helps distribute the weight you are about to place on it, and blocks any light from above.

3 Place your weights on the board. They ensure good contact between the exposure source, image and screen. You don't want light seeping in and creating fuzziness where there should be crisp, sharp edges!

Turn the light table on for 5–7 minutes. Resist the urge to lift the cover! You will ruin your print.

4 Turn the table off, and remove your screen. Always keep the light table off when not actually shooting a screen, and don't stare directly at the lit bulbs. It's not exactly the surface of the sun, but it's still ultraviolet light.

exposure times and you.

There's no way around it: trial and error establishes the exact exposure time for your individual light table. Timing is affected by the brand of emulsion, bulb intensity and number, and the distance between the bulbs and the glass. The light table in our studio is a massive, 6-bulb juggernaut that exposes screens in 4:20 flat. If you've made a light table from the instructions in this book, your exposure time will probably be very close to 6 minutes.

exposure without a light-table

We don't use this method in our studio, because it would take WAY too long for the amount of shooting and printing we do! Also, we like to use large screens, and this method works best for smaller images. However, it is easy to expose your screen without a light table. Just be prepared to experiment in order to find the right exposure time for the amount of light generated by your particular set-up. Here's the basic idea:

Place your screen on your table with the wooden edges facing up and the flat side down: think of the screen as a cafeteria lunchtray.

Now place your design right-side-up inside the tray. If your art has text in it, you should be able to read it.

Lay your piece of glass inside the tray on top of the art, and carefully weigh it down with the bricks, making sure they don't cover any part of your image! (This can be tricky, and is one of the drawbacks of the alternative exposure method.)

Turn on the lightbulbs and just walk away! Come back in an hour and turn off the bulbs.

now proceed to post-shooting hygiene

After shooting, remove your artwork carefully so that you can store in your image library for re-use.

Now comes the part I just love! You wash the unexposed emulsion off your screen and behold the negative image of your print! Amazing! You could sell tickets to this part! Place your screen in the wash-out tub. You can see a difference in colour between the exposed and unexposed areas of emulsion. If your design was on vellum when it was shot, you may notice a faint "vellum shadow" around your image; the emulsion is a

slightly different colour. This is perfectly normal. Vellum is translucent, not transparent, and so it blocks a tiny amount of light during exposure. The vellum shadow won't affect how

the emulsion washes out, or how the screen will print.

1 First, completely wet both sides of the screen with your spray-gun or showerhead

chip off the emulsion, especially if your design features a grainy image (when it's freshly exposed, the emulsion is still fragile). Now wash both sides again, and don't be timid. If you shot your screen correctly, it will be able to withstand lots of direct water spray. Keep it up until all the emulsion in your image area has washed away. I hold my screen up to the light to check if the mesh of the image area is completely clear; if it is, you get a pretty sparkling effect. If it isn't, how's the ink going to squish through when you print? Occasionally, you'll find a skinny line or so that just didn't work; I use a pin to etch those areas out. Make sure your screen is still wet when you etch, and hold the pin like a pencil so you don't poke a hole in the mesh.

Your screen must be dry in order to print with it. Speed things along by leaning it against a wall with a fan blowing on it for about 20 minutes. The screen is

totally exposed now, so light won't affect it any more.

How can you tell if your shoot was successful? It's devastatingly simple: All the emulsion washes out of your screen where you want it to, and none when you don't. The devastating part is when you need to tear your mesh out and start all over again! An over-exposed screen won't wash out enough; underexposure results in so much washing out that you lose detail from your image. If you're using a light-table, adjust your exposure time by 30-second intervals; use intervals of 10 minutes with the lightbulb method. It can be discouraging, but it's happened to all of us in the Peachy Silkscreen Community. Even if you're certain of your exposure length, here's a tip: don't shoot and dial. Not that I've ever messed up a screen by yakking on my cell and losing track of time…

attachment. This stops the screen from continuing to expose in regular light. ❷ Scrub each side with your scrub pad, concentrating on the image areas, but not too hard — you don't want to rip the screen or

are we there yet?

how to prepare your screen for printing

← **KITSCHY KITCHEN:**

I was pretty poor when I designed this print, but I needed real kitchen implements: my plan was to spraypaint them black, string them up with thread and photograph them from different angles. So I went down to my local thrift store, where they had a huge bin of basically unusable kitchenware. I had to bargain for a rusty potato masher! Who would want that except me? I loved the perspectives I eventually achieved with the photographs; it's traditional kitchen stuff, but it all appears to be floating in space.

scotch tape

① Once your screen is dry, tape all the edges of the frame, between the wood and the emulsion edge (where the mesh is exposed). This prevents excess ink from escaping during the printing process and marking your fabric. Remember, the "outside" of the frame is the side where the mesh is stapled flat; if you think of your screen as a cafeteria tray, the "inside" is the surface you would place your lunch on, with the sides rising up around it. If you have a number of images on your screen that you will be printing separately, tape around the one you plan to print on the inside of the frame, as close to the image as possible.

2 Hold the screen up to the light, and look for open spots of mesh that are not a part of your print. They will appear as little pinpricks of light. 3 Seal them over with a dot of nail polish, any colour you like (or any colour you don't like anymore, and want to find a use for someplace other than your be-nailed extremities). Let the polish dry.

Your screen is print-ready. Are you ready to mix some inks? Read on!

printing inks
a peachy primer

We use water-based inks for a number of reasons. They work best on natural fibres, like cotton or silk, which we prefer for our clothing designs. They're made with 100% organic pigments. They have a softer feel on fabrics (great for silks). They absorb into cotton-lycra stretch so that the print areas stretch too, and don't crack and flake off with wear. They don't smell and are non-toxic — especially important since our studio is in our store! They wash out easily from the screens with just plain water. And if all that doesn't convince you, consider this: to heat-set water-based inks after printing, let your printed item air-dry, and then just toss it in the dryer for 30 minutes or iron for a good minute on the highest setting. Finally, it takes very little time for the water-based inks to dry (5 to 10 minutes, so you can layer colours without the wait) and they're easy to mix, with only 2 ingredients (base + pigment = mixed ink).

mixology for silkscreeners

There are two types of bases that make up the volume of your ink:

Transparent base

→ Use for any colour ink on white or light-coloured fabrics.

→ This thin, clear base acts as an adhesive for pigment. You only need droplets of pigment to make one large plastic ice-cream container of ink — that's enough to print about twenty t-shirts!

→ Easier on your screen and won't clog it as fast as opaque ink (good for those easily-distracted silkscreeners, like me!)

→ 5 gallons of base costs well under $100 and will last a long time.

→ Black ink is made with transparent base, but you can use it on both light-coloured fabrics as well as dark-coloured ones. The black pigment itself is opaque.

the red menace.

Avoid disappointment! In our experience, you cannot make RED ink with OPAQUE base. It always comes out pink. Printing with red on black or dark fabrics does not work unless you print a white image first, wait for it to dry, and then print red ink on top of the white.

printing: it's not just for t-shirts anymore.

There's a whole world of printables out there. I've had students who printed glaze on clay tiles before firing. You may never need to buy a present again!

→ paintings
→ wrapping/tissue paper
→ wallpaper (already on the wall)
→ quilt squares — good for family photos!
→ socks and undies
→ blank book covers
→ jeans, skirts, coats
→ fabric posters — bands love these, because you can use fabric that's even cheaper than paper, and people will want to steal the final result (the ultimate tribute for a band).

And when you finally get around to printing t-shirts, think of the shirt as a framed piece of art; the negative space is just as important as the printed area. Reach beyond the front or back to those neglected areas: sleeves, around the sides, the neckline, the bottom edge. Try printing the shirt inside-out for a distressed, vintage look.

Opaque base

→ **Used for dark or black fabrics only** (red and royal blue are considered dark)
→ This is a premixed white base (transparent base + white pigment).
→ Depending on the colour you want, mixing with opaque base takes about three times more pigment than with transparent base
→ 5 gallons of base costs about twice as much as transparent, plus all the pigment needed, making opaque inks very expensive to use, but...
→ it makes really bright intense colours, like our famous hot pinks and lime greens
→ has a thick consistency, making it dry quickly — clean off your screen as soon as you finish printing!
→ White ink on any colour fabric, even white fabric, is always straight opaque base. (Transparent black ink on black fabric will result in a textural, tone-on-tone effect.)

all the printing that's fit to print!

What do you feel like printing on today? Cotton velvet, burlap, fancy handmade paper, old newspapers, cotton-lycra stretch (we use the kind with 5% lycra for our stretchy tops and skirts); all textures of silk; wood; canvas; camouflage; walls and ceilings; funfur…you name it, we've printed on it in the Peach Berserk studio. If it stands still long enough, we'll print on it. And just because you've printed on something already doesn't mean you can't layer another print on top! There's just one rule: the print surface has to be absorbent to some degree. That's why printing won't work on glass, or PVC. Use your imagination! Whatever the surface, experiment on a little piece — it'll either print or it won't. Finding out what doesn't work is just as valuable as discovering what does.

The material you've chosen to print determines how you need to set it up for the magic of the printing process. No matter what you print on, make sure there are no stray objects underneath it, like pins or loose staples. Their image will show up in relief if you print over them (although this might be a fun effect to play with)!

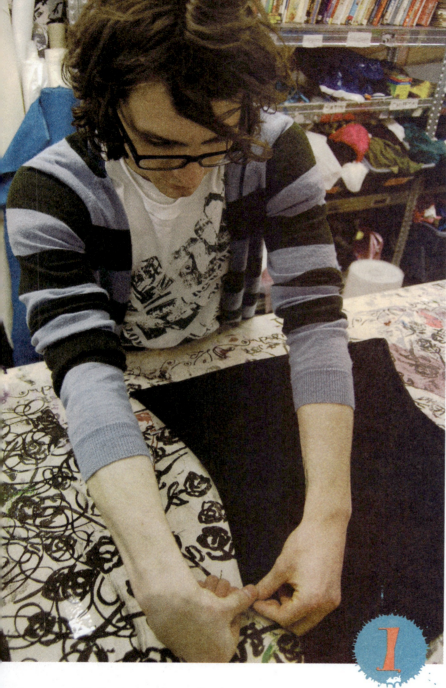

Lengths of fabric: stretch the fabric over your print table surface. Staple it down all around, sides and top, with about 12″ between staples. Pull the fabric tight as you go, to avoid wrinkles or folds that would result in a gap in the printed design.

T–shirts, other garments, pillowcases, messenger bag flaps: Flatten out the garment or area to be printed as much as possible, and ① pin it down with straight pins, inserting them on an angle with the point towards the middle of the item. The pins should lie flat, not stick up like tiny fenceposts — they'll catch on your screen. For a t-shirt, insert a piece of scrap paper inside the shirt to keep the ink from seeping through, and then pin the hem, underarm and top of the shoulder.Want to centre a single image on a t-shirt? Angle a single pin into the middle of the neck ribbing, at its lowest point where the ribbing meets the fabric on the front of the shirt. Only the head of the pin should show. Before you start printing, position your screen so that the top line of your image is centred on and about 3″ down from the pin head; you'll be able to feel it through the mesh for guidance.

Paper: Making your own gift-wrapping is just one of the ways to use printed paper. Try Japanese handmade paper sheets with embedded fibre, or print on paper bags! For big sheets, a single staple in each corner will suffice. You could also use low-tack masking tape (the kind painters use for taping off corners and trim) and tape around the edge of paper products; it will hold adequately and won't leave surface damage.

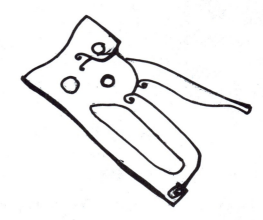

Close registration prints require a bit more preparation beforehand. If you are applying multiple layers of spot colour and want a precision-printed look with a minimum of overlap, you need to make sure that your fabric (or whatever item you are printing) doesn't lift up and creep around when you lift up the screen. Fabric adhesive is available in spray form where you buy your silkscreen supplies. Spray a thin layer directly on the canvas of your print table or pad before laying down your fabric and stapling or pinning it. If you're not picky about the colours overlapping, you can skip this step.

fabric, meet ink. ink, this is fabric

how to print

← BUNCHA ROSES:

This one is really hard to print to begin with, because it's such a close registration that if it's even a tiny bit off, the repeating print won't work. And to make it worse, it's really popular for wedding dresses, so of course the brides want white-on-white. That's almost impossible to achieve in our studio, because there's ALWAYS something that gets into that white ink... even a tiny fragment of dried black ink can ruin the fabric. Don't let a print challenge defeat you, though—for every disaster, there's a workaround. I've been printing white wedding dresses since the beginning, but I also thank the powers that be for goth brides!

things you will need:

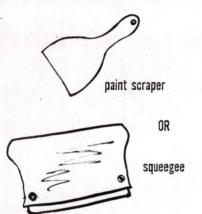

paint scraper

OR

squeegee

No matter what surface you've chosen to showcase your design, it's the beginning of a beautiful friendship. Take a few moments and breathe; time to print.

single images or small screens

1 Place your screen flat-side down over the area you want to print on. Place about a tablespoon of ink close to the image you're going to print, "inside" the screen.

Hold the screen firmly in place with one hand. **2** With a paint scraper, lightly drag the ink over the image — this is called 'flooding' your screen. Try to use the minimum amount of ink that will cover your image. Now scrape the ink from side to side or from the bottom of the image to the top.

③ Hold the scraper upright, near the base — you don't want to push any ink beyond your design area (also known as 'bleeding').

You can go over the image in both directions with the scraper to really cover the fabric fibres, but: **leave the screen in place until you have laid down an even layer of ink over the entire image to be printed.** You **must not** lift up the screen, even a tiny bit, to check your print, because no matter how careful you are, it will never regain its exact original position. You'll smear your print, and that's not what you came for (unless you're achieving a deliberate effect, in which case, smear away with my blessings!).

ink tips

For a random colour-wash effect, place a blob of two different colours side-by-side on the screen and scrape them together over the image. Or, change the colour of ink between prints without rinsing the screen. You have **too much ink** if it bleeds beyond the image on the printed surface. You **need more ink** when the image comes out faded — although it does give you that coveted vintage look.

④ Now, the moment of truth: lift up the screen by tilting it onto one side of the frame. There it is — your design, immortalized in ink. Isn't it incredible! And now you can do it some more! (Silkscreeners do it repeatedly, after all.) Lay the screen down CAREFULLY on the next item to be printed; now that there's ink on it, you only get one chance to position it. Reapply ink as necessary, and print like crazy. If you are printing images close to each other, cover the freshly-printed ones with scrap paper to protect them as you move the screen. You can always use the printed paper in a collage!

If you're like me and just can't wait to see results — or you can't be bothered with all that exposure business just at the moment — here are two ways you can print using a screen with stretched mesh, and no emulsion at all!

direct to print:
no emulsion, no exposure, no waiting!

1) Resistance ISN'T futile!

This method uses flat objects that will 'resist' the ink when you print. Your ink will squish through the screen mesh all around the flat object, which shows up as an unprinted area on the fabric.

Find or make flat objects to serve as the resist: cut shapes or letters out of cardboard; make a collage using existing shapes like leaves or lace; loop patterns in string… anything works as long as it is FLAT!

Staple or pin your fabric (or item to be printed, such as a t-shirt or pillowcase) to the printing surface.

1 Place the shapes directly on the fabric.

2 Lay your screen carefully over the shapes, and apply ink just as you would on an exposed screen, with a scraper or squeegee.

3 When you are finished printing, lift the screen, and carefully remove the objects you used to create the resist.

…and there is your fab print! SIMPLE!

2) Fill in the blanks.

You can also block out areas directly on your screen by using either masking tape or liquid screen filler, available in art stores. This method works just like the resist technique, only in reverse: your design will show up as an inked area surrounded by unprinted fabric.

Masking tape: apply the tape directly to the screen, on the side that will contact the print table. You are blocking out the area you want to leave unprinted, and leaving open mesh in a shape you want the ink to get through. Let's say you want to print a skull image. On the flat side of the screen, tape over the entire background of the skull, and place circles of

tape in the eye holes. When you're done, you'll see a skull shape in plain mesh, surrounded by a protective barrier of tape that the ink can't penetrate.

Screen Filler: This is a liquid that you can buy in the silkscreen section of art supply stores. 1 You just use a paint brush to paint the filler on your mesh

where you don't want the screen to print. It's exactly the same principle as the masking tape technique, but you're painting in the background of your design instead of blocking it out with tape. When the screen filler is dry to the touch, it will not wash out with water, and you can start printing with it!

You may be thinking, "Hey, I could combine these techniques and just put tape (or screen filler) directly on my screen in the shape of my design! Won't the ink just squish around it like in the resist method?" The answer is YES, you smart silkscreener! Full steam ahead!

silkscreening secret revealed

repeating prints are easy!

← MISBEHAVIN' MERMAIDS:

What knitting is to other people, cutting out shapes in rubylith is to me! I go into a trance and I just can't stop. I remember someone saying they could crack an egg at my house and there would be a bit of rubylith in it! "Misbehavin' Mermaids" is one of my first really complex prints. It's an interlocking design, so it's ideal for repeating prints on big lengths of fabric. I wanted the mermaids to be living my life if I were a mermaid: they're talking on the phone outside of their long–distance–plan hours while sneaking junk food from the fish. This print created itself as I cut it, and I worked on it for weeks. I've made hoodies combining this print with "Voluptuous Vegetables" and called them "Surf and Turf"!

save the fabric!

If the fabric we're printing is quite a bit wider than 40", we carefully cut off the extra width, and print it later. Why waste it?

Designing prints that repeat over yardage of fabric is one of my signature techniques, as well as one of my favourite ways to silkscreen. These designs are the ones that I shoot onto our large format screens and print 10 yards at a time on my aircraft-carrier-deck print table. (Seriously, it runs the entire length of the print studio. My daughter liked to get up on it and play fashion show when she was little). The secret is in the seamless way the image fits together as you print the same screen side-by-side until you run out of room!

I love teaching students how to design repeating prints, because it's much simpler than it looks — although once they learn how easy it is, I don't seem as smart as they thought I was! Here is my super-simple way of making a very impressive repeating print.

I make my designs so that the finished dimensions are about 40″ × 20″; this means that they will print on 40″-wide fabric, with the image repeating about every 20″. The fabrics you want to print will probably come in a variety of widths, like mine do.

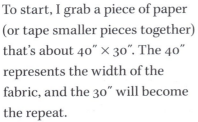

To start, I grab a piece of paper (or tape smaller pieces together) that's about 40″ × 30″. The 40″ represents the width of the fabric, and the 30″ will become the repeat.

1 Next, I draw or assemble my design down the middle of the paper lengthwise, trying not to stray too close to the edges.

2 Once the middle of my paper is designed the way I like it — I cut it up! I know it sounds crazy, but that's what I do…I take a pair of scissors, and I cut a path right through the middle of the designed area, lengthwise, taking care not to chop through any of the drawings. It's better if the cut line isn't straight, but meanders around the images a bit, making it harder to see where the repeats join up once the design is printed.

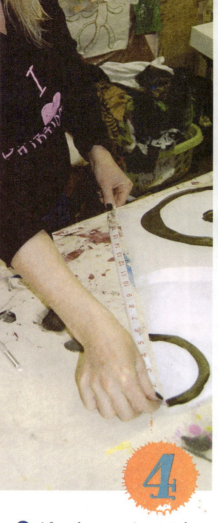

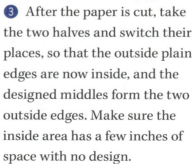

3 After the paper is cut, take the two halves and switch their places, so that the outside plain edges are now inside, and the designed middles form the two outside edges. Make sure the inside area has a few inches of space with no design.

4 With a ruler or measuring tape, ensure that the top edge and bottom edge of the repeat side are the same measurement. You may have to fuss with them a bit to get them the same, but once you do, tape it all securely together.

5

Now all you need to do is complete the design in the inside area, and voila! A repeating print. Rest assured that the outside edges will join up nicely, because they used to be attached.

Expose the design onto your screen according to the directions in Chapter 8.

repeating prints are easy ✳ 109

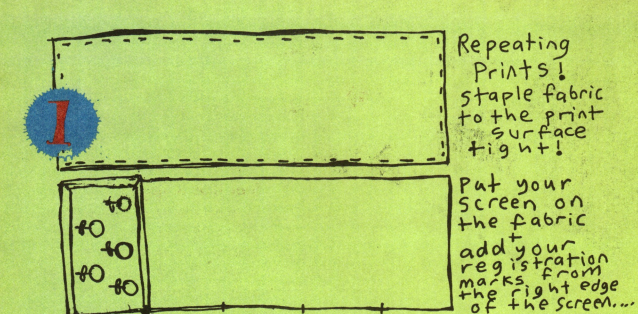

Repeating Prints! Staple fabric to the print surface tight!

Put your screen on the fabric + add your registration marks from the right edge of the screen....

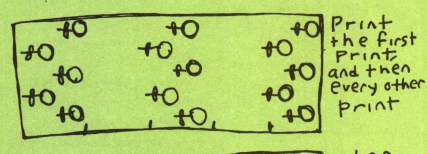

Print the first print, and then every other print

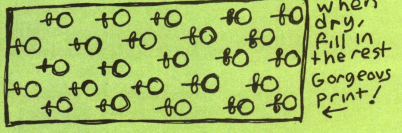

When dry, fill in the rest Gorgeous Print!

You have a repeating design shot onto your screen, and you have checked its registration measurement (see sidebar). It's almost printing time! This is where a long printing surface like the one I described at the start of the chapter really makes your job easier. The longer the print surface, the more efficiently you can print.

1 Staple your fabric to the print table, starting with the four corners. Make sure it's tight!

2

You also need to decide if your repeating print
will have a 'nap' — be uni-directional — or if it can
be cut in either direction. Keep in mind that a
uni-directional print makes it harder to cut out
pattern pieces for making into clothes, and will
therefore use more fabric for a single garment.

Keep the fabric taut, and staple
it down at about 10″ intervals
along the sides.

Place your screen at the left end
of the fabric, where you want to
make the first print. Don't get
out the ink just yet! You need to
make *registration marks*.

② Start at the lower right hand
corner of the frame. From that
point, moving to the right along

the fabric, measure out the length
of your registration measurement.
Make a small chalk or pencil
mark on the fabric at that point,
low enough that the screen won't
cover it when you start printing.
(Leave the screen where it is; you
won't need it for the rest of the
measurements.)

③ From that mark, continue
along the table, measuring out
the length of the registration

measurement and marking it as you go until you get to the end of the fabric. It's fine if your final measurement takes you over the end of the fabric; you will be able to print your repeating design right to the fabric's edge, and there won't be any waste.

Be sure to make some marks so that you can align your screen-frame horizontally as you print — we built our rectangular print table to suit our large screens, so we just line up the bottom of our screen frames with the edge of the table. If that system doesn't suit your printing surface or screen size, you can mark horizonal alignment points in chalk on your fabric, or draw a permanent straight line on your print surface where fabric won't conceal it.

3

Now you can make your first print! (General printing instructions are in Chapter 10.)

Start printing where you left your screen, on the far right side of the print table.

Carefully lift the screen up and move to the right along the print table. **Skip the first chalk mark**, and set the screen down so that the right-hand outside edge of the frame aligns with the **second** chalk mark. (We pass over that first chalk mark because if you were to set the screen down there, it would rest

on the wet ink of your first print! Not good!) You only get one chance to lay the screen down, because it has fresh ink on its mesh. See why the registration marks are so important? Print your screen, and carefully lift it up.

Now skip the **third** chalk mark, and line up your screen with the **fourth** one, and repeat in this manner down the table.

4 **After you print the last print, don't pick the screen up!** Just leave the screen in place on the print table until the prints you

4

have just done are dry to the touch. Cover the image on your screen with a thick coat of printing ink (we call this 'flooding' the screen) to prevent it from drying out while you are waiting.

When your first round of prints are dry, go back to the beginning and repeat the process to fill in the spots that aren't printed. This time you will use the odd-numbered chalk marks, and skip the even. You now have a stunning, long piece of fabric featuring your

own repeating print! Amazing, isn't it? Was that so hard?

Of course, you don't need to shoot a large-format screen to make a repeating print. This technique works on small screens too! Or, if you've got a single image or group of images that you love, you can simply print them over and over in a pattern. Try staggering an image into a brickwork repeat. Printing vertically gives you a photo-booth strip result. Or embrace anarchy and do a crazy overlapping repeat at random.

beyond the print!

Once you've printed your repeating design and it's dry, you can still take it a step farther. We like to handpaint some of our prints by applying printing inks with paintbrushes. The co-op students who work in my store love this part of their job. It's very important to heat set the entire fabric **before** and **after** you paint it. If you forget to heat set before painting, the design will run where the wet ink touches it.

ushes you up to her

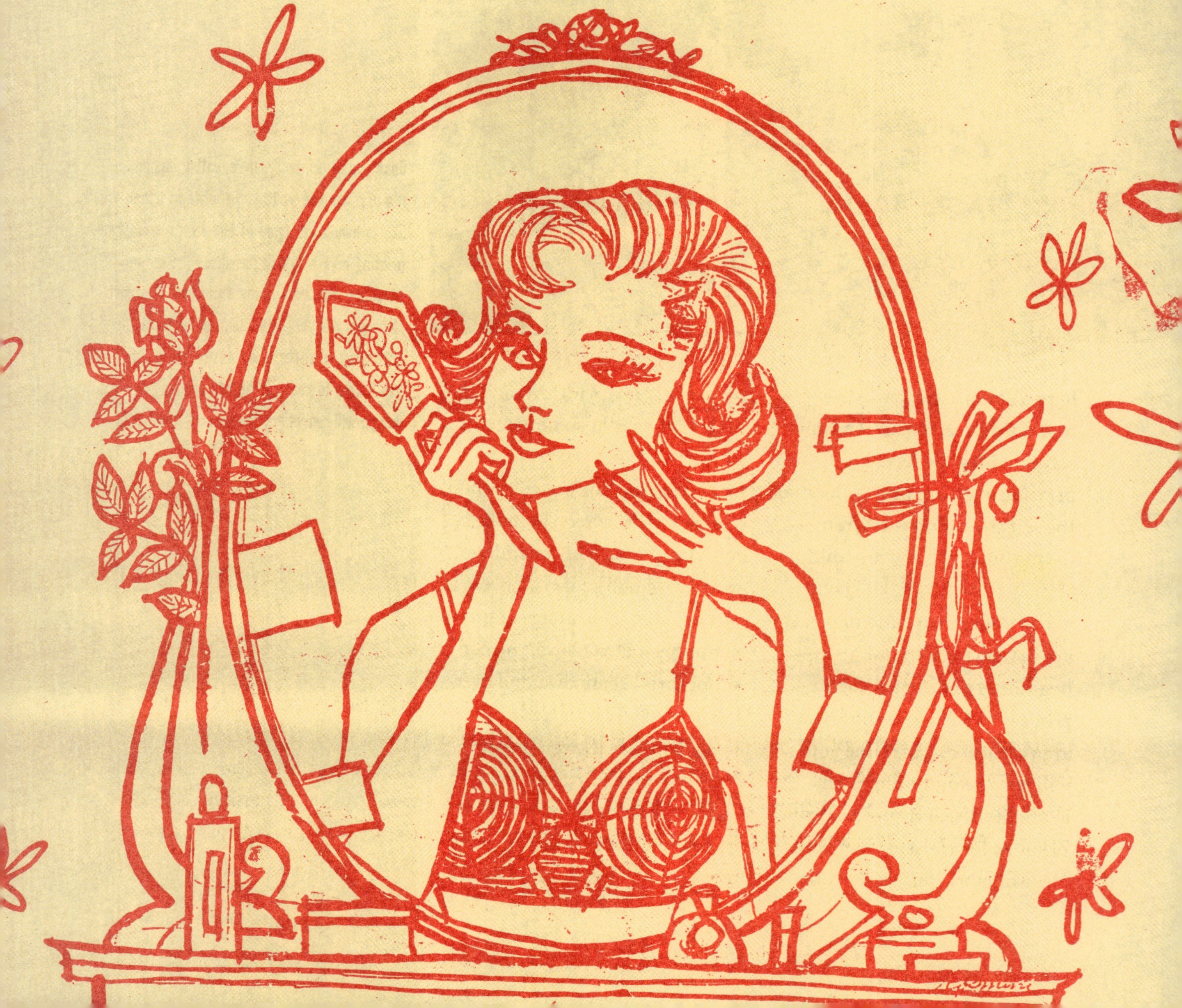

12

wash and set
final tips for lasting beauty

BRA-VO!

When I designed this print in the early nineties, there just wasn't anything like it. I had to dig for the 50's line drawings in piles of old fashion magazines and sewing patterns. (Today you'd just google, but this was the digital dark ages, remember.) For me, this print comments on past and present definitions of femininity. I like the way it celebrates women's bodies, damn the torpedo-bra, full speed ahead. I pulled it out of my print library to I could used one of its images on a promotional sticker (doubling as a business card) that's captioned: "Point Me To Peach Berserk, Baby." Its popularity with customers has fluctuated over the years, but for the right person, it's a perfect fit.

screen care

No matter what method you use to print, you will end up with a screen covered in ink. Now what? First of all, don't *ever* let the ink dry on your screen! Always rinse it thoroughly as soon as you're done, using the same care that you did when you washed out the emulsion: a medium spray until the mesh areas are clear again. If you're in a rush, you can wipe as you rinse. You'll find that the mesh area gets discoloured after use, but that's normal. Dry the screen well between print sessions, and store it where it won't get poked or dinged. Treat it with care, and your gorgeous screen will yield hundreds, maybe even thousands, of prints.

artwork care

No screen lasts forever. After the heavy use they get in our shop, our screens get damaged, or clogged with ink, no matter how tenderly we treat them — we do run a crazy, busy studio! You may find one day that your screen just isn't printing the crisp, complete image that you've come to expect. That's when you'll be glad that you stored your original vellum for re-shooting. We suspend our large-format screen designs from skirt hangers and store them on a clothes rack in the basement. I like to go down there and leaf through them when I need a quick review of what I've done in the past, or to check on how I accomplished a particular effect.

heat-setting your finished prints

All water-based inks need to be heat-set once they're dry, or they'll fade noticeably when washed. The easiest way is to take your finished items and toss them in a regular household dryer on HIGH for at least half an hour. Nothing will shrink, because nothing is wet — I promise. Don't worry if you don't own a dryer; I didn't when I started out. I would just stuff my gorgeous printed things in garbage bags and lug them down the street to the funky local laundromat — and I did that for *years*. Eventually, I bought a used dryer for about $200 and it works like a charm. You can also iron an individual image on the highest setting. Make sure to move the iron over it repeatedly, WITHOUT STEAM, for at least 3 minutes or so.

silkscreener's procedure review

part One

Stretch new mesh on screen

Coat screen with emulsion

Cure screen in darkroom

Part Two

Design your own print(s)

Prepare design to shoot on screen

Part Three

Shoot design onto screen

Wash out screen

Allow screen to dry

Part Four

Mix inks, pick fabric

Staple/pin down fabric

Print like crazy!

Part Five

Wash out screen

Heat-set printed fabric

Roller Coaster Curls

13

projects

some ideas for you to try

← GLAMOUR GALS:

This was never supposed to be a print, just a row of figures that could be individually cut out and used to fill in blank spots on printed fabric, or as overlays. I was designing a lot of patchwork items then, as well as a print of ornate empty picture frames, and I drew The Gals with those projects in mind. But the rows appealed to people when they saw the fabric on the print table. I kept hearing how it was such a good idea to arrange the ladies in simple rows, but what looked like my brilliant skill as a fabric designer was really just expediency. The names over the ladies' heads, like "Niagara Falls Hair", I drew on with a friend of mine while we were drinking beer at a café. The names were never meant to appear on the final product, as you can tell from the creative spelling. Glamour Gals is one of my oldest prints and is still going strong today. Beware: projects can take on a life of their own!

and now for your first print!

At first I wasn't going to put a project section in this book at all — because the whole point of learning to silkscreen is to make and print all *your* designs, the ones that are burning a hole in your brain. Think of these projects as helping you along the way to your own prints. They provide a chance for you to practice the techniques, and still end up with a cool item that you printed yourself. Do them in order, mix them up, alter them to suit your ideas — or ignore them altogether and just dive into your own stuff! I can't wait to see what you come up with!

before you do any of these projects, you need to:

→ Make a screen frame (Chapter 4)
→ Stretch mesh on the frame (chapter 5)
→ Coat your screen with emulsion (Chapter 5) — remember, don't store it for more than two weeks!

each project will involve different ways to:

→ Design your print

then, when your design is done, you will:

→ Prepare camera-ready artwork (Chapter 7)
→ Shoot your design onto your screen (Chapter 8)
→ Prepare your printing surface (chapter 4)
→ Prepare your inks (chapter 9)

and start the printing party!

easy projects
hey presto, you're done!

hands-on towels

Ink applied to hands makes a great image for silkscreening onto handtowels for the bathroom or kitchen. Towels can't look dirty if they're already stamped with prints! Kids love doing this project. You can capture their tiny hands and feet forever on your screen, and reprint them on different projects whenever you like.

Time to get those hands dirty.

techniques to practice
→ photo-emulsion printing with a single image
→ positioning of an image/motif

project-specific materials:
→ hand towels (the choice is yours: recycled; new; all cotton or poly/cotton blend; plain or pre-patterned; even smooth or terrycloth. It all works!)
→ non-toxic, waterbased paint in a dark colour
→ little hands and/or feet!

1 Apply a dark-coloured, child-safe paint to your designated hand or foot, **2** and carefully print onto plain paper. Do lots of these for maximum choice (Caution! Tickles may result!) Select the image that you like best, and photocopy it onto vellum. It's possible to skip the photocopy stage if you use India ink, because it's already opaque, but it can be difficult to clean off little hands and is better suited to older children or adults.

Shoot your design onto your screen (full instructions in Chapter 8).

It's almost printing time! Pin each towel to your print surface, as many as will comfortably fit side-by-side (see full instructions on preparing your item for printing in chapter 9).

③ Position your screen over each towel so that the individual image you want to print lies directly over the area you want it to print on. ④ Apply ink with a scraper (full details start on page 99, Chapter 10).

When you are finished printing, carefully lift the screen. You don't have to stop with one image per towel. If you are feeling adventuresome and confident, use a piece of scrap paper to protect the freshly-printed area and print another image next to it, or overlapping it. If you're concerned about ruining the print, or aren't sure about where to place the next one, then take a moment away. Go on to the next one, or if you've already applied one image per towel, then wash out your screen and let it dry before making your next application of ink. This is also a good idea if you are changing colors between printings.

5 There is no rule as to how much (or how little) of the towel you can print. That's part of the beauty of silkscreening. And you can store your screen and use the image from it for something entirely different: a journal cover; your jeans; a lunchbag...

6 Once you're happy with the way the towels look, let them dry to the touch, and then tumble them in a dryer on HIGH heat for about half an hour to heat-set the ink.

no comment vintage outfit

Silkscreening your wardrobe is addictive, so don't blame us if you
end up printing a comment, or an essay, on everything you own!
Experiment with different typefaces on your computer, or go old-
school and write by hand. We found a vintage cardigan and
slipdress that were cute on their own, but much more fun once we'd
Peach Berserked them. By printing "Fashion Victim" on the hem of
the dress, and "I'm Too Hot In This" on the sweater, we added a DIY
twist on a classic bombshell look.

techniques to practice

→ printing with typefaces
→ printing on irregular surfaces

project-specific materials:

→ vintage clothing items of your choice

① Decide on your phrases and play with different ways of typesetting them. If you like the handwritten look, you can use india ink and write directly onto vellum (this will save you the photocopying step). For a fun, edgy look, try cutting out individual letters from different print sources, and arranging them like a ransom note. Whatever approach you decide to take, the final step is to photocopy your text onto vellum. Be sure that the text is the size you want for your print; you may need to enlarge it on the copier. (See chapter 7 if you need more details on how to prepare camera-ready art).

Shoot your text onto your screen (full instructions in Chapter 8).

Now, prepare your clothing for printing. Flatten out the area you're planning to print, and pin each item onto your print surface (see full instructions on preparing your item for printing in chapter 9).

② Position your screen that the phrase you want to print lies directly over the area you want it to print on. ③ Apply ink with a scraper (full details are on page 99, Chapter 10). Your print can overlap pockets and seams if you like! You'll have to press HARD on those raised areas to get consistent coverage. You can

also try printing "off the edge" of your garment (say, the hem or the cuffs), but don't cut off too much, or the phrase won't be readable.

When you are finished printing, carefully lift the screen. If you want to repeat the phrase, use a piece of scrap paper to protect the freshly-printed area and go right on printing the next image!

4 Once you're happy with the way your new outfit looks, let it dry to the touch, and then tumble it in a dryer on HIGH heat for about half an hour to heat-set the ink. Remember, nothing will shrink because the clothing isn't wet, so it's OK to heat-set a wool sweater, for instance.

Now go get changed and make your statement to the world!

intermediate projects

that wasn't so hard!

techniques to practice

→ photo-emulsion printing

→ printing the same image multiple times

project-specific materials:

→ bedsheets or other cheap fabric (this can be recycled; new; all cotton or poly/cotton blend; plain or pre-patterned… it's up to you!).

bedsheet band poster

It's less expensive to silkscreen your own band posters onto cheap fabric than to get large-format photocopies! If it comes to that, cut up old bedsheets (and if you're a musician, or dating someone in a band, it WILL come to that). In terms of design, this is the time to go wild. The juxtaposition of bizarre, obscure found images that have nothing to do with the band will grab people's attention. One musician in my silkscreen workshop threw in a vintage illustration of a kid punching a clown-shaped punching bag!

Design your band poster (see Chapters 6 and 7 for the full scoop on designing your print!). If you want to make it re-usable for different events, leave a space for specific date and venue information on the main image. You can make another screen and print that information separately, or even hand-write it in permanent marker, if you're not doing very many posters.

Prepare camera-ready artwork (full instructions in Chapter 7).

Shoot the design onto your screen (full instructions in Chapter 8).

Prepare your bedsheet for printing. (For more information on preparing your fabric for printing, see Chapter 9.) If you have a large surface to print on, it's best to staple the entire sheet down and print as many images as it will hold. ❶ Simply lay the screen down, apply the ink with a scraper, ❷ lift the screen up carefully, and

lay the screen down next to your first image. It's that easy! ❸ ❹ Repeat until you run out of room. Once the entire sheet is dry, you can cut it into individual prints. If your print surface is limited (a portable print pad on your kitchen table, say), it will be easier to pre-cut the sheet into

3

pieces, pin down each piece separately, and print one poster at a time. Be sure you have somewhere safe to lay out the printed pieces so that they can dry to the touch undisturbed (a clothesline would be ideal, but an unoccupied section of floor is fine too). Cut all the pieces ahead of time, so that you can keep up a rhythm: pin down, print, remove print to dry, repeat.

4

You can always add a bit of extra visual appeal by handpainting detail on your finished prints (depending on your musical statement, it could be anything from red paint blood splatters to puffy glitter ink).

Once they are fully dry to the touch, heat-set your finished posters in a dryer on HIGH for 30 minutes. This will help the ink withstand the weather once you staple them up around town.

132 ✳ silkscreen now!

supplies party! art apron cut-offs

Now that you're a silkscreener, you need those art supplies holstered for quick access! If you're like me and forget to put the supplies back into their pockets, at least this apron will let you know what used to be in there. This is the artist's version of the change aprons that restaurant servers wear. It requires no sewing experience whatsoever. If you can use scissors and sew on a button, you can make this apron — I guarantee it.

techniques to practice

→ preparing camera-ready art with photocopied three-dimensional objects

→ photo-emulsion printing

project-specific materials

→ a pair of old jeans, at least one size larger than you usually wear

→ a large button

→ sewing needle and thread, any color

→ black spray paint (optional)

→ a variety of art supplies, like brushes, craft knives and blades, markers, calligraphy pen and nibs, eraser, pencil, scissors

1 Cut the legs right off the jeans — just at the point that all the seams meet at the crotch (take care not to cut through the pocket linings). This part is like revenge on an unflattering wardrobe choice: *Take that! And that! You will never make my rear look huge again!*

2 Leave the side seams intact, and cut all the way up the back seam and through the waistband. **3** You will now have a roughly rectangular piece of denim fabric, with all the jean pockets still attached. Lay this aside for now.

It's time to experiment with photocopying your found objects — the art supplies. If you have a scanner and printer (separate or as a single unit), you can use them instead of a copier. Take the things to your local do-it-yourself copy shop if you need to. And just start photocopying — onto plain paper at this point (this is a

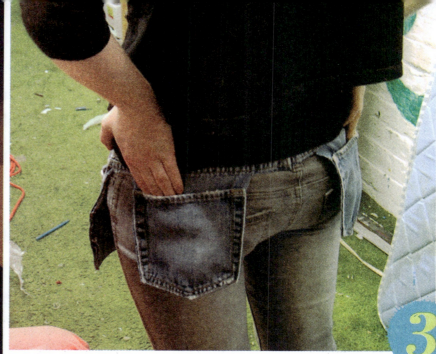

good time to re-use discarded pages). Look for different ways to display the objects: open up the scissors, splay the bristles on the brushes, arrange the nibs into a circle like a blossom, break the pencils or sharpen them to get the curly shavings. If you find that the objects are printing out too gray, you may need to spraypaint them black before copying to give them more contrast. Remember that you can manipulate these photocopies images if you like:

digitally, or simply by enlarging or shrinking them on the copier.

Select your favorite images, and photocopy them onto vellum (see chapter 7 if you need more details on how to prepare camera-ready art). You will be printing these images individually onto your apron, so don't worry about what goes next to what at this point. Just remember that you need to leave about an inch of space around each object.

4

Shoot your design onto your screen (full instructions in Chapter 8).

It's almost printing time! Pin the denim rectangle onto your print surface (see full instructions on preparing your item for printing in chapter 9). Tape around each image on the screen, so that you won't accidentally print part of its neighbor.

④ Position your screen on the denim so that the individual image you want to print lies directly over the area you want it to print on. Your print can overlap pockets and seams if you like! Or you could line up just the upper portion of a brush, say, with the top of one of the pockets to make it look like the brush is sticking out of the pocket. ⑤ Apply ink with a scraper (full details are on page 99, Chapter 10).

⑥ When you are finished printing, carefully lift the screen. If you are feeling adventuresome and confident, use a piece of scrap paper to protect the freshly-printed area and go right on printing the next image. If you're concerned

5

about ruining the print, or aren't sure about where to place the next one, then take a moment away. Wash out your screen and let it dry before proceeding with the next image. This is also a good idea if you are changing colors between printings.

There is no rule as to how much (or how little) of the apron area you can print, and you don't even have to use all the images on your screen on this particular project. That's part of the beauty of silkscreening — you can store that screen and use an image from it for something entirely different.

Once you're happy with the way the apron looks, let it dry to the touch, and then tumble it in a dryer on HIGH heat for about half an hour to heat-set the ink.

Now for the finishing touch: cut a horizontal slit with a craft knife into the middle of the waistband, just a bit smaller than the diameter of the button you have chosen. Sew the button on the opposite side of the waistband. And there you have it! Try your apron on, jump up and down and yell "Supplies!"

techniques to practice

→ cutting designs from rubylith

→ photo-emulsion printing

project-specific materials

→ a pair of pillowcases (100% cotton, poly/cotton blend, or even satin for truly high-voltage romantic effect!)

→ photographs of the happy couple (black and white are best, such as photobooth strips)

hopeless romantic pillowcases

Do you hate shopping for wedding gifts as much as I do? They're so expensive, and let's face it, dull at best and redundant at worst. Why not give an utterly original, personalized gift, and practice your silkscreen skills while you're at it? Start with a photo of your favorite happy couple, and trace their faces by cutting them out of rubylith. Cut out the pet names they have for each other for an even more unique touch (this works even better if the names are sexy, private ones). Print one face and name on each pillowcase, and give them as the most individual and fabulous wedding gifts ever.

Select photos that don't have too many mid-tone shades. You may need to photocopy them to increase the contrast, but a reasonably high-contrast black and white image will be easier to work with and increase the impact of the final print. Try to find a pair in which the faces are roughly the same size; if you have to scale one up much more than the other, you may lose vital details. Follow the instructions in the sidebar on pg. 74 to achieve high-contrast results in photocopying.

Once you're satisfied with the images, lay a sheet of rubylith over each one, and cut a design that follows the contours of the faces. You can emphasize certain features on each if you like, or go for a more balanced, realistic effect. If you're not totally sold on the romantic theme, this is your big chance to add a pirate eyepatch or twirly fake mustaches! (Full instructions for rubylith are on page 71.) If you like, you can cut names or phrases out of rubylith, or typeset them separately and photocopy them onto vellum before you shoot your screen.

Shoot your design onto your screen (full instructions in Chapter 8).

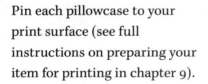

Pin each pillowcase to your print surface (see full instructions on preparing your item for printing in chapter 9).

② Position your screen over each pillowcase so that the image you want to print lies directly over the area you want it to print on. Apply ink with a scraper (full details are in Chapter 10).

When you are finished printing, carefully lift the screen. If you want to print both sides of the pillowcase, make sure to let it dry to the touch before turning over, re-pinning, and printing the other side.

3 If you like, embellish the final prints: try colouring in the eyes, adding lipstick and blush, or highlighting the hair.

Once the pillowcases are dry, tumble them in a dryer on HIGH heat for about half an hour to heat-set the ink. They're now ready for a long and happy relationship, and if it doesn't work out, well — they're easy to rip into dust-rags for personalized revenge!

techniques to practice

→ designing with charcoal
→ printing with the screen held vertically

project-specific materials

→ vintage picture frame(s)
→ finishing nail(s)

on-the-wall art

This project lets you indulge in a forbidden activity from childhood: applying ink to your wall. It's just as much fun now as it was then! This project encourages you to experiment with drawing charcoal in the design stage. When you're ready, you silkscreen your image directly onto the wall of your choice. Finish by hanging a strategically-placed vintage frame, and you have wall art. This project works on wallpaper as well as on paint.

1 position, but you can certainly use a larger screen if you prefer. Line up a friend to help hold it steady when you print.

1 Experiment with drawing in charcoal for your design. I chose to do female nude studies, because I never get tired of drawing them. Charcoal suits the long, flowing lines of the nudes particularly well.

Select your favourite image (or series of images, if you are doing more than one), and photocopy onto vellum (see chapter 7 if you need more details on how to prepare camera-ready art).

Shoot your design onto your screen (full instructions in Chapter 8). We used a t-shirt size screen, because it was easier to handle in the vertical printing

2 One of the joys of this project is: there's almost no preparation of your print surface! All you have to do is decide where you want to print on your wall. If you're not certain of your ability to center the image by eye, measure first and draw some lines in pencil to help guide you when you print.

3

you were printing horizontally (full details are on page 99, Chapter 10).

When you are finished printing, carefully lift the screen.

④ Proceed with the next image if you are printing a series.

If things haven't worked out exactly as you planned — your screen moved a tad, and blurred

③ Position your screen on the wall so that the individual image you want to print lies directly over the area you want it to print on. Hold the screen very

firmly — you will only get one chance to make this print! Get a friend to hold the screen for you if you prefer. Apply ink with a scraper, just like you would if

the image, perhaps — all is not lost. Let the print dry to the touch, and then over-print it with another colour. (Wash out your screen and let it dry before proceeding with the overprint.) You could also add a touch of hand-painting or other embellishment to disguise any little flaws.

When the printed area is dry, use a finishing nail to hang your vintage frame so that it shows off your new art to its best advantage. Remember that the image doesn't have to be centred in the frame! Don't forget to sign your work — you'll want to take all the credit.

techniques to practice

→ printing from a photograph
→ drawing with pen and ink
→ cutting shapes in rubylith
→ applying spot colour

project-specific materials

→ cotton canvas
→ pillow stuffing
→ tassels for trim (optional)

family portrait redux

People who take my silkscreening workshop are always bringing in family photographs and asking if they can make a print from them. Of course! I do it all the time; it's a great way to explore your heritage and challenge yourself artistically. This project shows one of the ways you can take a family photo beyond the usual T-shirt or paper print. You make a series of identical prints on cotton canvas, vary them with spot colour application, print a line of text across them and... cut them into individual prints! When you sew the canvas into little ornamental pillows and place them side-by-side on your couch, you'll be able to read the writing across them. Magic!

Select a family photo that doesn't have too many shades of grey. You will photocopy it to increase the contrast, but a reasonably high-contrast black and white image will be easier to work with and increase the impact of the final print. Faces are always a good choice; small figures with a lot of background, less so. Follow the instructions in the sidebar on pg. 74 to achieve a camera-ready result.

1 Lay a sheet of rubylith over the final image, and cut a design to emphasize certain areas. Think of how you want to vary the prints from frame to frame. Add colour to clothing by cutting out a skirt in rubylith, for instance, **2** or cut out the hair shape to change the colour of the person's coiffure! Full instructions for rubylith are on page 71.

On a piece of vellum, use a pen and india ink to hand-write a line of words that will appear across the final framed images. It could be the title of the piece, or a favourite quotation, or even a date spelled out in words.

If you have a large enough screen, you can shoot the photo image, the rubylith, and the words on vellum on the same one. If not, you will have to shoot multiple screens. Remember that there doesn't have to be very much room between the separate items on the screen; ½″ or so will suffice!

projects ✳ 147

3

Pin or staple the cotton canvas onto your print surface.

3 Print the photo three times, side by side, leaving enough canvas between them to create the sides of each pillow. Be sure to not to smear the first prints with the wet ink on your screen;

you can carefully lay a piece of scrap paper over the freshly-printed canvas to protect the image while you print the next one. If you have shot all your images onto one screen, wash the screen and let it dry between printing different elements.

4

4 **5** When the photo prints are dry, print spot colour over the photos using the rubylith layer. If you are using different coloured inks, you may want to wash out your screen and let it dry between applications — or just let the colours bleed into each other.

5

6 When the spot colour is dry, you can print the line of text over all three images. Remember that some canvas will be lost to seam allowance (the part that gets hidden through sewing), so if you want the text to appear across the front of the image only, you will have to pre-measure and print the text in sections.

6

When all the layers of printing are done, carefully cut the canvas into individual prints. Cut plain canvas in the same size to create the back of the pillow (or use contrasting fabric like velvet or satin!). Place the right sides together and sew the seams, leaving a hole on one side so that you can pull the finished pillow right-side-out and stuff. Sew the hole closed, add tassels at the corners, and arrange them on your couch!

challenging projects
think of the bragging rights

techniques to practice
- → planning a more complex project
- → precision printing in different colours

project-specific materials
- → fabric for tablecloth (or recycle an existing tablecloth)
- → off-white organza

inviting the prints for dinner

This is a way for you to adapt my "Fashion Plate" print to suit your own gourmet taste — and to explore an alternate method of making a repeating print. You'll design two small screens for this project: one is of an empty place setting, with plates, knife, fork and spoon. You'll repeat this print at each "place" on a fabric tablecloth that fits your table. The other screen has the food you're serving — and you'll print this on placemats made from rectangles of see-through organza. The plates show through beneath the images of the food! It's not just dinner — it's art!

Measure your dining table, and cut your tablecloth fabric to fit. We used cotton gingham, but any fabric will work, patterned or plain. Measure and cut your organza placemats. (You can hem all of this fabric now, or wait until the project is complete. We left our placemats unhemmed, because I liked the frayed edges.) If you have a tablecloth that you never use, this is the perfect time to upcycle it!

Lay the cloth on your dining table, and plot out where the placesettings will go. I cut pieces of paper the size of each placemat, arranged them to see where they looked best, and then pinned them onto the tablecloth. Don't skip this step, or you may end up with a printed placesetting that hangs off the end of the table! Although that would be fine if you're inviting Salvador Dali, I suppose.

① Design your placesetting print. I drew mine in pen and ink, because I wanted a contrast between the flowing lines of the placesettings and the photographic realism of the food prints on the placemats.

Design your food print. ② Make sure you check it for size against the plate you've drawn in the placesetting print — the dinner shouldn't overflow the plate. Be

3

open to experimentation! I used vintage food advertisements, and at first I thought I would feature meatloaf. When I photocopied it, it just looked like a big dense lump (much like real meatloaf, come to think of it). I found a chicken leg that looks much more appetizing!

4

Photocopy your designs onto vellum (see chapter 7 if you need more details on how to prepare camera-ready art).
Shoot each design onto a separate screen (full instructions in Chapter 8).

3 4 5 To print the tablecloth, pin or staple it onto your print surface. The paper placemats you pinned down earlier will guide you as you print. Remove each piece of paper just before you print a placesetting.

5

6

⑤ To print the placemats, pin each one securely to your print surface. Now apply your ink, using a different squeegee for the each different colour of the food items. We did green for the beans, brown for the drumstick, and black for the outline of the potatoes. This is precision colour printing!

You can do all the colours in the image before moving on to the next placemat, but you must be very careful to avoid mixing the inks and making mud-coloured food. If this happens, wash out your screen and let it dry before proceeding.

Once all the printed fabric is dry to the touch, heat-set everything in a dryer on HIGH for 30 minutes. Iron the placemats so that they lie flat.

Now set your table, light the candles, and pour yourself a celebratory drink!

techniques to practice

→ collage using found images on a theme
→ repeating print

project-specific materials

→ vintage magazines
→ silk fabric
→ fringe (optional)

not your great-auntie's silk scarf

The old lady's printed silk scarf is a fashion stereotype. Here's a project that shatters the stereotype by using a crazy collection of unusual vintage images. I searched through magazines from the 40s and 50s for images advertising items for the elderly. The resulting collage is anything but demure, and printed on a scarf it becomes a commentary on how society perceives aging and fashion. And it's a repeating print, which can be applied to a considerable yardage of fabric, so maybe a "Not Your Great-Auntie's Sexy Cocktail Dress" is next!

Decide on your theme, and source your images.

Follow the directions for making a repeating print design in Chapter 11

Shoot your screen (see Chapter 8).

Print as much fabric as your print surface can hold! Staple it at all four corners, then around the edges, holding it taut.

1 Print according to the directions in Chapter 11

the

inspiration

for the print!

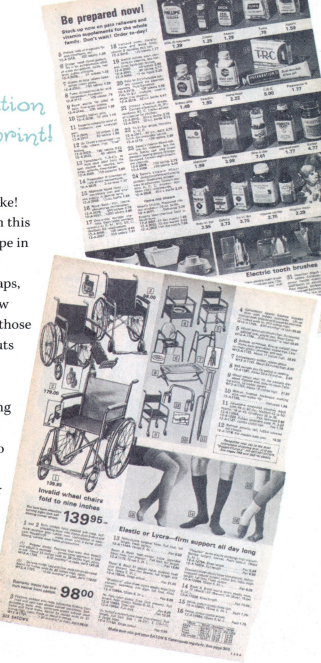

When the fabric is dry, cut it to size. For a scarf that's printed on both sides, double the fabric over and sew it inside-out into a tube, then sew the ends of the tube shut, leaving a small hole so that it can be turned right-side-out (this is a lot quicker with a sewing machine, but you can do it all by hand too). Carefully sew the hole closed by hand, and iron flat.

If you prefer a scarf that's printed only on one side, just cut it to size, turn the edges in, and hem all around by hand or machine. Iron flat.

2 Sew fringe on if you like! You can do anything with this material! Change the shape in the double-sided scarf directions, stuff with scraps, and you've got a silk throw pillow (I stuff mine with those styrofoam packing peanuts sometimes!). Make table runners or curtains. Depending on your sewing skill level (or that of your friends who are willing to help), you could make boxer shorts or a skirt, or re-line a vintage jacket.

Why do women earn onLy 62% of what men make?
Ludicrou
and we work twice as hard!
Some StiLL dont believe ina
How

epilogue

← LADY LIBBERS: THE LAST WORD.

I love all my prints, but this one has a special meaning for me. I used pictures of women from 1950s catalogues and patterns, and you could just **tell** they were supposed to be saying things like "I would **never** let my man come home to an untidy house!" or "He really **does** know best, dear." It was, well, liberating to encourage other kinds of conversation in the speech bubbles I drew: "I'd rather be curvy" and "How come men are go-getters, but we're bitches?" Women's issues are very important to me, and in this print I literally make it my business to be a feminist. I've had ongoing and overwhelming customer response to this print, from women and men of all sizes and ages, ethnicities, orientations and backgrounds. People really relate to it; they want to wear it and give it and talk about it, and that makes me feel like I've made a difference to a cause I believe in. With your new superpowers of silkscreening, you can do the same!

oh no! what happened?!

troubleshooting guide

Too much emulsion washed off my screen.

The exposure time wasn't long enough. Increase it in 30-second intervals if you're using a light table (half-hour intervals if you're using the hanging light-bulb array).

I can't get the emulsion to wash off where my design is supposed to be.

The exposure time was too long. Decrease the exposure time in 30-second intervals if you're using a light table, and half-hour intervals if you're using the hanging light-bulb array.

I printed my item but the ink faded the first time I washed it.

The ink may have been insufficiently heat-set. Allow your item to air-dry first, then tumble it on HIGH in a dryer for at least half an hour, or iron over the image for at least 3 minutes on HIGH without steam.

When you mixed your ink, you could have used too much pigment and not enough base to adhere to the fabric.

I printed my first colour but it smeared when I applied the second.
Let the ink dry to the touch between printings.

Everything's taking too long to dry!
A directional fan is your best friend. We have four big standing ones in the studio.

If you don't wash your screen thoroughly enough after printing, it will take longer to dry!

My inks have dried out. Can I rescue them by mixing in some water?
Unfortunately, no. Make sure to seal your inks well between uses. If it's just a bit hard, you may be able to strain out the chunks by squishing it through a scrap of mesh.

My prints come out looking blobby.
You're using too much ink — and/or you may not be holding the screen steady while you print.

My prints come out looking patchy.

You're not using enough ink. Also, you may not be applying the ink consistently. Use a scraper that is a similar size to your image, and remember, it's okay to scrape ink over the image more than once.

I can't get fine detail in my print.

This could be a problem with your initial image; try making some of the fine lines thicker by enlarging the image slightly or going over the lines with pen and ink. It could also be that your exposure time isn't long enough, and therefore too much emulsion is washing out.

My screen tore!

Argh! We feel for you — it happens to all of us. Sorry, but you have to start again. The screen can't be patched once it's been stretched.

My print based on a photograph doesn't show enough detail.

Too many grey tones! You need more contrast in the initial image. See page 74 for tips on how to achieve it.

There's too much variation from print to print.

While some variation is part of the handmade nature of silkscreening, sometimes you want to minimize it. In that case, try to keep the amount of ink consistent from print to print; make sure that the item you are printing is securely attached to the print surface (use fabric adhesive as well as staples/pins); and keep the screen motionless during printing.

now it is YOUR turn to get printing!!!

xo Kengel

acknowledgements

Ingrid Paulson, whose expertise and assistance in every aspect of the project has been invaluable; Debbie Stoller, who believed from the beginning; the wonderful staff at Peach Berserk; models Nicole, Chantelle, Vitus, Jessy, Letitia, Rebecca. Kingi's daughter Digby. Rick and Ann Carpenter for early editing help and encouragement; Nicole Brayshaw-Bond and Jocelyn Lee-Bun for Photography; Wendy Rombaugh; Vinh Huynh; Rusti Moffat; Sharon Bailey; Janet Murie; Java House; Midtown Reproductions; Young & Young.

Our friends and family: Gillian Carpenter; Betty Danowski; Judy Evans; Kallie Garcia; Deverne Jones; Joe, Trish and Katie Lindsey; Kath Sharpe; Greg Sweitzer; Norbert Mantik; Louisa McCormack; Judy Blumstock and Ellen Beth Rosenthal.

index

MEET THE AUTHORS

Kingi Carpente...
fashion designer who ca...
into a silkscreen print. ...
print studio and store o...
West, she has command...
fans for over twenty yea...
through silkscreen work...
business seminars and ...

...ki (right) is a writer,
...terature — and
...ddict. She still wears the
...rom Kingi back in 1994.